FAR HORIZONS

Adventures at Sea

6-01-16

To:
Sue,

Welcome aboard our yacht!
true adventures,

Enjoy these
Have fun!

Elsie Mackie

Elsie Mackie

PRESS

CONTENTS

Chapter 1

Conflict Arises

J im announced in a loud voice, "Elsie, we're buying a yacht, selling the house, and leaving the United States for several years." My husband startled me with his plan.

I gasped and my mouth dropped open in shock. My thoughts whirled. *Is he kidding? How did he come up with this crazy idea? This is January. We can't do this. The children are happy. Alan's in second grade. Alicia's due to start kindergarten in the fall.*

I pushed back tears with my hand as I choked out the question, "What about the children?"

Jim retorted, "We'll teach them aboard our yacht."

I swallowed my words. Jim attempted to persuade me as I backed into the kitchen. I groped the edge of the counter to steady myself. *We had everything a family could want: a nice suburban home, happy kids, good friends, nice church, and a better than average income. Why this wild idea?*

I caught my breath as I reasoned. *He's forty years old. Maybe he's in a mid-life crisis. I have to encourage him to see his doctor.*

"Jim, has your shoulder been painful? Should I make an appointment for you with Dr. Hoffberg?"

Jim replied, "Yes, talk with him and make an appointment for me. Find out what vaccinations will we need for going to other countries?"

Oh, no, he is serious. What does he mean leave the United States for several years? I took another deep breath and let the air out slowly before I answered him. "I won't endanger the children. We can't disrupt their lives. I am staying right here."

Two days later, Jim left for his appointment with the doctor to get the results of his physical examination and blood tests. His brown hair and blue eyes presented a nice-looking man with the beginning of a receding hairline.

The smell of homemade bread permeated the house as I worked on dinner in the kitchen. I bustled about checking the beef roast in the oven. I used the hand beater to whip cream for the cherry pie. I wanted Jim to have a special dinner tonight after he saw the doctor. When Jim got home, he walked into the living room, sat on the ottoman. "Elsie, come in here. I need to talk to you."

I wiped my hands on a dishtowel as I left the kitchen. Jim looked up as I walked toward him. He hesitated.

"What did the doctor tell you? Are you hurting? I made your favorite dinner." I leaned over and kissed my husband.

"I paced the floor in his office and kept grabbing my right shoulder trying to stop the pain. I know my face was contorted. The doctor told me that my blood chemistry tests are normal, and that I have all the symptoms of a mid-life crisis. I have bursitis in my shoulder. He gave me a cortisone shot to help reduce the pain. He encouraged me to do exercise rotations with my shoulder to keep it loosened up. Oh, I have to avoid milk products."

"I'm restless. I can't sleep. I lose my temper easily. I don't want to work. My stomach bothers me. What next? I've torn up card decks before, but I didn't mean to scare you when I knifed the cribbage board."

. I countered, "You *did* scare me. When you lost, it wasn't necessary to take it out on the cribbage board."

He continued, "I'm fed up with working. I've decided that my dream to go cruising is *going to happen.*"

Again I was stunned and stared at the floor. I gulped and blinked back tears. Finally, I glanced up at him. "We can't afford to leave. What about the children . . . the house?"

Jim raised his voice, "You *will* go sailing with me. I'm going to buy a yacht. I'll sell this house. Alan and Alicia will like sailing." He glared at my face in defiance.

I clenched my fists and retorted, "I won't do that. We can't be irresponsible."

Jim frowned as he slammed his fist on the sofa. He glowered at me and insisted, "I'm selling this house. You can either go with me or shake hands with the new owners."

I backed away . . . "You can't sell it without my signature!" *What's happened to him? His actions frighten me! Why does he keep yelling?*

Jim changed tactics. "The sailing lessons we took in Berkeley in the small El Toros sailboats were fun. You were the only woman in a class of eleven men. You didn't capsize your El Toro when the rest of the class did. Remember years ago when we talked about how amazing it would be to sail around the United States?"

I reflected, "Yes, day trips were fun when we didn't have children. Sailing on fresh water lakes or even in San Francisco bay was different. We're settled in a comfortable home now. We have wonderful neighbors and good friends. Alan is doing well in school. Alicia is too young to be put into an unstable environment."

Jim pleaded, "This is the only time to go, before friends, school and church activities crowd into their lives."

I steadied my hand on the desk as I tried to absorb his idiotic plan. I shriveled inside. I had surrendered to my husband our entire married life. My hands shook. *Why isn't he hearing me? It's taken years for us to save up enough money to get Jim through the University of California and get his degree in Industrial Engineering. I worked to put him through school. We should have equal say in major decisions.*

Jim stood, walked to the screen door and pushed it open. He smoothed back his hair with a hand. He frowned, then turned and pointed his finger at me and blurted, "You will learn to be a first mate. My dream to cruise the seas is going to happen!" The door slammed behind him.

"Dear Lord, Jim's never treated me this way. We usually discuss plans before any drastic changes are put into effect. He's acting in haste. He's only thinking of himself. He's pulled the rug out from under me this time. I am *stunned* by his actions. What should I do?"

The next day I drove to my best friend's house. I rushed out of my car, dashed through the gate, and pushed the doorbell. My friend, Mary Lamski, thirty-five, opened the door. Her sweat suit matched her black, curly hair. Her brown eyes stared at me. She questioned, "What's wrong? Did someone die? Are you hurt?"

Mary ushered me into her spacious entry hall, then down to the newly renovated kitchen. I collapsed into a chair and trembled. Sunlight beamed through the skylight into the kitchen. Live plants with yellow and blue flowers lined the window box. *I hoped that she had a good answer as to how I could get out of this dilemma.*

My words spilled out, "Jim's been brooding about our house like a frustrated rooster. He wants to sell our house and leave the United States to live on a yacht! It's not fair to the children."

Mary shook her head and her eyes widened. "That's crazy. You told him you wouldn't do it, didn't you?"

I hung my head. "Yes, says he's going to get a buyer for our house."

Mary lowered her voice. "Jim shouldn't ask you to give up your home to leave our civilized country to sail to some unknown areas. God help you! Elsie, you've spoiled your husband for years. You jump to wait on him. Cracking his soft-boiled eggs for him, I wouldn't do it. You're like a Japanese housewife. You're endangering the children and yourself." Mary shook her head from side-to-side. Her brown eyes punctuated her words. "Now is the time to say: no!"

I reflected, "The last time I remember being on the ocean was off the coast of Mexico. I vomited and had diarrhea. The boat captain turned the fishing vessel back to the harbor due to rough weather. He was sick."

Mary shrugged her shoulders. "Doesn't Jim know the dangers involved in a life lived on the ocean? Don't consider this, Elsie."

I sighed and shook my head. "I thought Jim loved me. He never seemed unhappy before. Why now? He changes the rules when the rules don't suit him."

Mary gawked as she put her hands on her hips. "You're not going to give in to him, are you? This time you'd be going too far."

I stared at Mary with my mouth open. "I hoped you would understand. I love my husband and our kids. It's because I love him that I give in to his wants. I choose to trust God for direction. I promised to love, honor, and obey my husband. People don't really mean that vow anymore, but I did."

I returned home. Alan and Alicia read books in their bedrooms. The original wrought iron divider with the grape clusters set the family room off from the dining area. The wood crackled in the fireplace. Jim seemed calm. He smiled and gave me a hug. "Let's eat in here by the fireplace. It's more romantic." He kissed me on the lips and ran his finger down my cheek.

He spoke softly, "There's less work living on a yacht. It's beautiful sailing in the moonlight."

I cooed, "I've been happy living in California. Our children's friends play well together. Our block parties and church activities fill our need for friendship, and you have business friends."

He held me in his arms and continued his pitch. "You know, honey, if I were a millionaire, I'd want to go cruising. Let's do this while we're young enough and have our health."

"A change like this is monumental. I feel responsible for our kids. What if we *lose* one of them overboard? What about their education?" I pleaded. Then I pulled away from his embrace.

Jim insisted, "Listen to me. It'll be educational for the kids. We'll teach them the phonics system. We'll have life jackets, safety harnesses, life rafts, a medical emergency kit, and you're a nurse."

The next day, I drove to the shoreline, then jerked the car to a halt and parked. I wandered to the cliff's edge. Waves crashed against the rocks, gulls shrieked, and clouds covered the sun. A powerful wind gust pushed me toward the ledge. I argued, "You can be so violent, with your waves and your stormy wind. You terrify me . . . how can I live with you on a yacht? You're not fair to the children. All you know is that you get what you want. How many sailors, how many ships, how many dreams have succumbed to your will? How many lives have been lost?"

Tears poured down my cheeks as I headed for home to get dinner ready before my husband arrived. Forty-five minutes later, Jim walked in the front door. He called to me as he entered the living room, "I'm home. What's for dinner?" He paused. "Guess what lessons we'll take when we move to Florida?"

"Chicken and dumplings with tossed salad. I made your favorite apple pie this morning." I played for time. "What lessons?"

Jim hugged the children and kissed me on the cheek. He removed his tie and sport coat.

Jim laughed, "I've thought of everything. Scuba diving lessons, of course."

"Why would we take scuba diving lessons?" I questioned.

"It'll be fun to see what's in the ocean. Besides, what if the anchor chain or a line gets entangled, or if we need to check the rudder or hull?" His words were fixed on his goal.

I sighed and collapsed on the sofa. "*What?* I'm a nose breather! I like to swim where I can see what's in the water . . . in a swimming pool. I know I can't be a scuba diver." "I can't breathe through my mouth," I blurted.

Jim gazed at me. He paced the floor.

"Jim, when I was three-years-old, I played in the shallow water at Deer Lake in Minnesota. I sat on a nest of large *bloodsuckers*. I screamed for help. I remember hitting the water with my red pail and splashing water on my sister, Ruth. She was eight- years-old and picked the bloodsuckers off me. *It was horrible*." I shuddered from the memory.

Jim resolved, "We're taking scuba lessons."

I pleaded my case. "I *can't* breathe through my mouth. I nearly drowned when I was seven-years-old. I jumped off the end of a dock and tumbled in Pokegama Lake in northern Minnesota. I somersaulted underwater and couldn't get up. I opened my eyes and saw one brown leaf drifting slowly down underwater. As I watched this leaf, I *knew* it was the end of my life."

Unimpressed, he retorted, "You lived, didn't you? You *will* learn how to scuba dive."

There seemed to be no alternative from being locked into an uncertain future with a determined man who wanted to cruise the world in a yacht.

Jim grinned, "This will be the adventure of a life time." He rubbed his hands together in excitement. His plan went into action. "I'll start looking for a yacht," he said, and walked from the room without his dinner.

I walked to the bedroom and sobbed. I undressed and slipped into my robe. I blew my nose and wiped my tears. I reached for the Bible and opened it at random. I stared at the page in shock as my eyes found a verse from Psalm 139:9-10 and I read it. *If I take the wings of the morning, and dwell in the uttermost parts of the sea, even there shall thy hand lead me, and thy right hand shall hold me.* A deep peace flooded my entire being. God would be my protector, strength, and peace.

The next day, a sunny Saturday morning, Jim coaxed the children near the tree house he had built for them. They tossed a ball back and forth. Our backyard with a large doughboy swimming pool, redwood deck and evergreen trees boasted the largest lot in the subdivision.

"Son, how would you like to catch great fish in the ocean? And live on a yacht? Why, Alan, you'd be the boatswain."

I watched as Alan stopped tossing the ball, put his hand to his chin and cocked his head, "Daddy, what's a boatswain?"

"A boatswain is the ship's officer who is in charge of the sails and rigging. It's a big job, but I'll teach you."

Alicia watched and listened to her dad and brother as she climbed off the swing. Jim spoke softly, "Want to go sailing with daddy?"

"Can we go up and down?" She tossed her red hair and ran toward him.

Jim waved both arms as he smiled. "Oh, yes, up and down, lots and lots of times."

"Is that a big job, too? What does it mean?" Alicia crinkled her nose.

Her dad replied, "Putting the fenders out keeps the yacht from getting hurt when we dock. We'll call you, Cookie the fender tender. It's a very important job."

On Monday morning Jim dressed in his business suit for work. Then he kissed me and the children. He asked, "Elsie, what do we need in a medical kit? Get one assembled. Contact the local elementary school for the textbooks and lessons needed."

I nodded and took notes on a notepad. "I'll contact the children's doctor about their vaccinations and I'll contact Dr. Hoffberg about any shots that we'll need."

Jim smiled. "Check on our passports. We need to get the children passports although Alicia is so small she may need to be included on your passport."

I added this to my list. "You must have started planning this last year. There's so much to do. Children, I'll call you when your breakfast is ready." My heart pounded as I thought about the uncertainty of living on a yacht at sea.

Jim searched from California to Washington State for many months as he looked for the right yacht. He went to boating shows, different marinas, scoured the ads, and talked with cruising sailors. He told me, "I want one that is sturdy, so I pound the coach roof with my fist. I'm looking for a bargain."

Jim took a plane to Florida. He called, "I've narrowed choices and settled on a yacht with a center cockpit. This will give us as parents an aft cabin for privacy. The one I picked is a fiberglass Cascade 42. It's a sloop-rigged yacht that's in dry dock in Fort Lauderdale." He flew back to California.

"Look at these pictures of our new home! It's fiberglass yacht in Florida. She's forty-two feet long." The sloop was white with blue canvas sail covers. She appeared beautiful from the two photos we held together.

"It's got cool tiny round windows," Alan said. "Where are we going?"

"Those are called ports," Jim explained. "You open them from inside the main cabin. I sold a rental property to pay for the yacht. We'll sell our house before we move to Florida."

Alan and Alicia went outside to play in the fort in the backyard.

"Elsie, I think we should change the name of the yacht. It was called *Golden Dredge II*. I want to change the name because the previous owner was shot and injured off Columbia, South America."

My eyes widened and my mouth gaped in shock. I shuddered. "Jim, this is dreadful. We can't live on a yacht that has had tragedy. Isn't this an ominous sign for sailors to change the name of a vessel?

Jim continued, "He sailed with his family and they played musical instruments aboard. He did survive, but had to be airlifted out. He's unable to sail anymore."

That evening, Jim walked in carrying an armful of cruising magazines. He put them on the coffee table. "Elsie, here are some sea wife articles for you to read." Then we ate dinner and watched a television show as a family.

Jim said once the television was off. "Okay. Listen up! Who wants to name our yacht? Alan and Alicia, you each get one vote. Mom, you get two votes. I'm the Captain, so I get five votes."

Alan spoke up, "Dad, that's not fair."

Each of us volunteered different names for the yacht. "I like the name, Flying Cloud." Alan beamed at his choice.

Alicia chirped, "No, let's name her Princess Ann."

I chose next. "Let's call her Far Horizons."

Jim insisted, "Fancy Free suits me." The winning name selected was *Far Horizons*, since Jim decided to give in to me for a change. He continued, "Since I chose the yacht, your choice of the name seems right."

Three months later, our collection for the children's schooling grew. California textbooks, phonics workbooks plus the SCORE reading program necessary to teach Alan and Alicia for 3-4 years were stacked on our dining room table. I packed my favorite silver pants suit so at least I'd have one nice outfit to wear.

We received our passports, vaccinations, and started to shut doors behind us. Our house was sold. Alicia did have to sit on my lap for our passport photo since she was small.

Jim shared, "Elsie, today I turned my clients over to Dick and Mary Wilson. I've put my real estate license on inactive for four years. I've given power of attorney to Mary Wilson over our business affairs. I've packed my business papers and office equipment. Mary told me that when we need money, that she'll wire the funds via the Thomas Cook Agency. She also said that they intend to visit us in Florida before we sail."

Jim continued, "Bellinger Property Management will handle the rentals. I trust Dick and Mary to check on any mail, pay bills that come in after we leave."

Our friends gave us a going away party. "You are crazy for doing this, Jim." Several of our friends were airline pilots. Our bon voyage card read: This time you've gone too far. Gene Lamski wrote in our farewell card: Jim, this should give you a new angle for selling real estate. Elsie, you have my sympathies. Happy sailing to both of you, Gene

A sold sign was staked into the lawn in front of the MacGregor house. A moving sale was in progress as buyers carried off furniture, dishes, pictures, children's stuffed animals and toys. My beautiful car, a green Datsun, was also sold.

A U-Haul trailer hitched to Jim's Buick stood loaded with bathing suits, casual clothes, a medical kit, dry packaged food, canned food, plastic non-skid dishes, games and treats for the children, boating and school supplies. We said goodbye to neighbors and pulled away from our former house and started the drive across the USA from California to Florida.

"Are we in Florida?" Alicia asked nearly every hour. "Dad, can we get a cat to have on our yacht?"

Jim didn't answer.

We stopped to visit our friends, Connie and Phil Harris in Colleyville, Texas. We stayed overnight with them. Alan and Alicia had the opportunity to play with their daughters, Cathy and Debbie. Connie and I were distraught about this endeavor. "Elsie, I can't bear to see you leave. It's like the devil is dragging you off. Is there anything I can do to help?"

"Continue to pray for our family, Connie. I trust you. You are strong in the Lord. I'll keep in contact with you by mail and give you our address as it changes." We sobbed as we hugged one another goodbye.

We continued to cross the southern part of the United States only to stop for fuel and food. Jim announced, "We're here in Fort Lauderdale, Florida. I'll drive us to see *Far Horizons,* our new home." We were being pushed us forward into unknown territory.

Chapter 2

Dry Dock Dilemmas

Jim instructed us as we rolled into the marina. "Our yacht's in dry dock. We have to unload our belongings, and return the trailer to the nearest U-Haul facility."

The dry dock was in a swamp area. Our forty-two foot sloop, *Far Horizons*, stood ready to receive her new owners. She looked impressive with her six-foot keel braced on wooden stands. A ten foot ladder leaned against the hull.

Alan jumped out of the car and shouted, "Wow! She's great. Let's climb up and explore." He bolted up the ladder. "Dad, where do I sleep?" We all followed as he peeked through the hatch and into the main cabin. He flopped on the different berths, not waiting for his dad's reply.

We unloaded kitchen supplies, clothing, tools, and school supplies from the trailer and up into the yacht. I walked into the main cabin and lifted the lids to the storage bins. I commented, "Jim, there's water in all of the storage bins. The portholes are open. Where did this water come from?"

He sulked, "I forgot about it raining when I was here three months ago. I left the portholes open to air it out."

I was surprised that he admitted such a mistake.

I shook my head from side-to-side. "Okay, kids, help Mom bail the water out of these storage bins. We can't unload anything more until we have these bins clean and dry." We sponged the last of the water out of the storage bins. I washed the inside of the bins with clean, soapy water.

During the three months since Jim had returned to California, tiny bugs had invaded and hatched inside the main cabin. Now the bugs descended on our family with vicious bites. We slapped our faces, arms, hands, and legs. We felt the bites, but couldn't see the insects. The insects were inside the yacht and outside in the dry dock area.

"Quick, get the insect repellent! Rub it all over your exposed skin." I told the children. "Let me help you put it on. Don't rub your eyes with it." The bug-infested yacht overwhelmed me. Within minutes welts developed all over my arms and legs. The children received several bites, but not as severe as mine. Jim seemed impervious to the insects. He shrugged his shoulders and walked away down the dry dock pathway. He muttered, "The rest of the family seems okay." He didn't seem to care.

The following day, I counted fifty bites on one foot alone. I used band-aids to cover the large welts on my arms and legs. I rubbed my swollen eyelids with a clean tissue. "Jim, I'm allergic to these bites in this hot weather. I'm dizzy and nauseated." These nickel-sized, swollen red areas itched fiercely. I couldn't go outside for any length of time even with insect repellent on my skin. Sick, hot, and disappointed, I struggled to keep a brave outlook.

Alan and Alicia played hide-and-seek around the other yachts in dry dock. Alicia wore matching yellow shorts and tank top. Jim ordered, "Alan, come here and crush these empty boxes."

Alan decided that the best way to get the job done was to jump off the ten foot ladder. Alicia watched him and wanted to join in the fun. Neither realized the danger. She fell after following her brother's lead as she jumped off the ladder to crush the now empty cardboard boxes from our move. This forced her to hit her head against a large wooden brace that supported the next yacht.

"Don't tell Mom or Dad how you got hurt!" Alan warned. Of course, I heard him.

Blood gushed from her cut. Alicia held her head and cried, "Help, Mom, I'm hurt!" Tears flowed down her cheeks.

Alan watched and took a deep breath. He scoffed, "Ah, it's not that bad."

Alicia's eyes blinked, "I'm bleeding. But it hurts. Mom, help me."

I washed Alicia's face with soap and water. Then I cleansed the cut with hydrogen peroxide. "This will sting some, but it will kill any germs. I'm closing the cut with butterfly sutures. These are a special way to close a wound using tape." I shut the medical kit and hugged Alicia. "Alicia, I love you. You'll be all right. The cut will heal in few days."

Alicia replied, "Thanks, Mom. I'm glad you're a nurse."

On Tuesday morning, Jim announced, "Okay, family, today we start to scrape the barnacles off the hull and keel. Then we'll hose the yacht down with water."

Alan asked. "What's a barnacle, Dad?"

"Okay, family, come outside and I'll show you these barnacles." We climbed down the ladder with scraping tools in our hands. "See all these hard shells attached to our hull? They attach themselves to rocks or to the bottom of boats and ships. The hull needs to be clean so our yacht will sail faster. Tomorrow we'll paint the hull up to the waterline with a reddish protective coat of paint. On Thursday, *Far Horizons*, will receive a fresh coat of white paint above the waterline with a two inch blue stripe."

"Children, wear your oldest clothes 'cause it'll be messy work." We mustered energy as a team until all the barnacles were gone.

On Friday, Jim reminded me, "Oh, Elsie, once *Far Horizons* is in the water, we're taking those scuba diving lessons."

Oh, no. I'd forgotten about the lessons!

The water tank had been filled with fresh water in dry dock. Groceries and boating supplies were purchased and loaded aboard. Our excitement started when the yacht was launched into the Fort Lauderdale water network. *Far Horizons* looked beautiful in the water. The fuel tank was filled with diesel. Jim brought our yacht around to the city dock. A propane tank was brought aboard for cooking.

One of the first purchases Jim bought for me was a hand cranked portable sewing machine. He explained, "Honey, look what I bought for you. This is to mend clothes or to mend sails. Here are some heavy duty sewing needles and heavy thread." This was an antique sewing machine. Mending of sails had to be done while seated in the center cockpit for enough room for the sail to be spread out. Sewing would have to be done in a harbor when an anchorage was calm, but never at sea or in bad weather. I sighed and tried to figure out my husband's motives.

Why had I agreed to go with him on this venture?

Jim had taken a navigating course in California. He bought a sextant and learned how to take sun shots by measuring the distance of the sun to the earth's horizon during the day. At night he measured from the stars to the earth's horizon to locate the position of our yacht when at sea. I asked, "What happens if the sky is overcast or what if there aren't any stars out to plot our course?"

He reasoned, "I'll wait until the sky clears up." He continued, "Listen up, family. I'm teaching you some new words that are important. A fathom is a length of six feet. A fathometer measures the depth of water. Our keel is six feet so we must have more sea water than that to be safe. Two fathoms are also dangerous as the waves can hide reefs or rocks." He demonstrated how to read the fathometer which was immediately inside the starboard side of the main cabin.

Captain Jim purchased a small compass with a rubber ring around it. He said, "We can take this in our dinghy or emergency raft. It will float." He handed the compass for each one of us to examine.

"Alan, I want to explain to you some other important words. RDF stands for radio direction finder. This is a special marine radio which establishes the bearing of the station whose signal it is receiving. I'll be using it when needed. There's VHF, which means very high frequency. It's for radio transmission. There's a Coast Guard channel 22a, and channel 16 for distress signals."

Jim ordered, "Sea water will be used for washing dishes, and cooking when we're out at sea. We'll also use sea water for washing clothes and taking baths unless we're in a port. Fresh water is for drinking."

We had no refrigeration. Canned meats, canned vegetables, and fruits were stocked. Cans of dried food (such as green beans, apricots, bananas, and beef) were purchased as backup. Powdered skim milk and canned milk for the children found a place in the galley. Packages of dried yeast were added to make fresh bread, pizza, or cinnamon rolls when out at sea.

Fresh cabbages, potatoes, and onions put in net bags were tied on the safety rail inside the main cabin. In our hold we stored fifty pounds of rice, sixty pounds of all-purpose flour and thirty pounds of sugar. These basics were sealed in five gallon plastic buckets with tight-fitting plastic lids and secured with lines in the hold across from our diesel engine. There was a small passageway from the main cabin where one could crouch down under the center cockpit to get to the aft cabin. This would be dangerous to crawl through when out at sea.

"Jim, we need some fresh vegetables so I'm going to grow alfalfa and bean sprouts. I've learned that they will thrive if they're kept in a jar with a cheesecloth over the mouth of the jar. I'll secure the cheesecloth with a rubber band. They need a dark place. I'll put the jars in the bottom cupboard in the galley. Every few days, I'll rinse them with small amount of fresh water and drain the water off." I began to feel a bit creative.

We purchased non-skid plastic dishes with a design of the continents on them. A steel thermos for hot liquids was also a must. I reported, "Jim, I heard from one of the cruising women that Joy liquid soap works great in seawater. We can use it for washing clothes and dishes."

Jim decided, "Okay, great. Let's buy two used bikes to use when we are on shore. We'll secure them on the deck. We'll get a small charcoal grill also." This seemed like the extreme version of preparing for a camping trip.

We selected a Guest Log which had three columns: Date & Port, Name & Address, and Hailing Port. September 3rd 1976 we were still tied up at city dock where we took showers with our bathing suits on and hosed each other down.

Our first guests were Jerry and Birgitte McKinney with their son, Mark. Their yacht, *Xcaliber*, hailed from Washington, D.C. They docked their yacht next to us, so we became good friends.

September 14, 1976

I met Pastor Dennis Bupp who visited us at our yacht on three different occasions. He dedicated Far Horizons to our Lord Jesus. I took Alan and Alicia, plus a neighboring boy who was Jerry and Birgitte's son to Sunday school and church a few times while we were in Fort Lauderdale.

September 18ᵗʰ

Gene and Mary Lamski plus their daughter, Lisa visited us from Pleasanton, California. How great to see close friends again.

September 23ʳᵈ

Jim's Aunt Ella and Uncle Dave Keith from Fort Lauderdale came aboard for the first time. Dave had retired from Ford Motor Company in Detroit, Michigan.

November 8ᵗʰ

Dick & Mary Wilson came aboard to visit us from San Leandro, California. They stayed three days.

Jim's Aunt Ella and Uncle Keith invited us to dinner at their home before we set sail. Ella gave me a diary titled "Travels Abroad from S.S. QUEEN MARY" of the Cunard White Star Line. Ella suggested, "Elsie, why don't you write in pencil so if the paper gets wet, the writing won't smudge."

I started my diary in pencil: November 12, 1976 1:30 P.M. Overcast and warm. We tacked a zigzag course against the wind until we arrived in Miamarina in Miami, Florida at 10:30 P.M.

The next morning, our family walked into a marina supply store where we saw three kittens and a cat lying on an oval rug at the entrance to the store. Alicia said, "Daddy, I want a kitten." She bent over and picked up a gray and white kitten. She oohed, "Isn't this kitten soft. She likes me, I know it." Tears welled up in her eyes. She looked up, "Please, daddy. I need this kitten."

Jim relented, "Okay. You'll have to take care of it."

The store owner said, "These kittens have been weaned from their mother."

Later on I questioned, "Jim, why did you change your mind? Remember how you used cat traps to catch stray cats to turn them into the S.P.C.A. when they wandered onto our yard in Union City?"

He said, "Maybe this one will calm the kids down."

Our starboard lifeline had completely severed at the bow connection. The port light did not work. "Is this yacht safe?"

Chapter 3

Bahamas Exploration

On a remote island, in a small building with only a few shelves of packaged goods we selected some dry cereal. When we got back to our yacht, and opened the package, the cereal was loaded with bugs so we had to throw it away. I bought a chicken (I thought) on another island, marinated it, and boiled it for a long time. Jim retorted, "We expected a treat. We can't sink our teeth into the skin, let alone eat it!" There was better success with the fresh grapefruit, bananas, plantains, and coconuts bought from the natives.

I learned to improvise, and shifted to the foods that were available. Plantain fritters became a favorite recipe with our family. The plantain is a type of banana where the skin must be black or it's not ripe. After the skin is peeled, the plantain is sliced and dunked in batter, then fried. Another alternative was to sauté the plantain slices in butter with a dash of salt.

Out at sea, I made fresh bread almost every three days. I used the same no-knead recipe for making pizza and cinnamon rolls.

The meat from inside the conch shell was very tasty in conch salad and fried conch. Conch shells were abundant in the Bahamas. Octopus, goat meat, squid, and manta ray were tried and then scratched off the menu list. Fish eyes and snails were my daughter's favorite snack. As for fish eyes, Alicia said, "Mommy, they taste like bubble gum."

I posed the question, "Jim, I'm concerned about Alan's sleepwalking. Remember when he sleepwalked at home in California? He picked up my new sewing material in his hands, and laid the material over his arms. Then he walked into a bathroom and turned the water on over the material. What if he walks off the yacht at night?"

"One of us will be on watch in the cockpit or if we're in a harbor moored out, our son will wake up when he hits the water." Jim grinned.

He has an answer for everything.

I read in my devotional book: A wife is responsible to her husband. Her husband is responsible to Christ. I took a long, deep breath. "I may die going with Jim. Lord Jesus, you're my refuge and my strength. You are my ever present help in trouble. I trust you to rescue us daily. Thanks."

Alan took the hard dinghy out by himself for a short ride in the bay. The little outboard motor fell off. He dove over the side, came up for air, and sputtered. "I can't find it. What am I gonna tell Dad?" He climbed back into the dinghy and rowed back to the yacht. He looked wet and scared. He took several deep breaths.

Jim sat in the cockpit as he read a book. Alan climbed aboard. He blurted out, "Dad, something happened."

Jim asked, "What? Are you okay?"

Alan admitted, "I lost the outboard." He gulped. "It fell overboard. I can't find it." Tears formed in his eyes.

Jim got up and shouted, "I told you to be careful. What the hell were you thinking? We're going to go look for it. Get back in the dinghy."

Jim rowed back to the area where the motor fell off. He tossed out a small anchor, and both dove over the side.

Jim complained, "It's too deep. I'm afraid it's gone. Hell's bells, you're a pain in the ass. I need to get another small outboard before we can leave."

Alan apologized, "I'm sorry, Dad. The motor must not have been on tightly enough." He hung his head.

Jim shook his head in disgust and didn't answer. Alan rowed them back to the yacht. Jim tied the dinghy painter to the cleat. He shoved Alan forward onto the deck. He called, "Elsie, Alan lost the outboard! We can't find it. Have to spend the money for another one."

Alicia piped up, "You didn't! Glad I wasn't with you. Mom showed me how to read numbers."

I put my hand to my forehead and sighed, "What next? Alan, you take too many chances. I worry about you."

Alan shrugged his shoulders,.

November 28th

We left No Name Harbor at 4:20 A.M. and by 6:40 A.M. there were over one hundred fathoms of water under our yacht. By 2:15 P.M. Bimini was sighted. Alan was seasick and regurgitated. I gave him half a tablet of marezine and dry crackers which seemed to calm his stomach. *I hope Alan doesn't get appendicitis. I am not a surgeon.*

Alicia was happy and sang to entertain herself. At one point, she accidentally knocked our small charcoal grill overboard. She shrugged her shoulders and said, "Oh, well, it was in the way." This was the end of any chance of grilling.

We sailed to Gun Cay and by 4 P.M anchored in Honeymoon Harbor for the night. The next morning, I strapped my knife around my right ankle, and put on my B.C. vest, fins, mask and snorkel. I jumped off the side of our yacht to explore the warm and crystal clear blue and green water. Alicia and Alan swam into shore where they found conch shells, a yellow fan shell and a large piece of sponge. Jim set an anchor underwater at 8:40 P.M. The tide went out. The depth read one fathom as our keel bumped the bottom of the ocean floor.

November 29th

We left Gun Cay to Cat Cay to clear customs in the Bahamas. We went back to Gun Cay and snorkeled. We saw three leopard rays, small barracudas, and many schools of small fish. The different color patterns on each school of fish dazzled us.

8:30 P.M. Small craft warnings were issued along with a storm warning. Our Danforth anchor was cast astern. Jim was up at 2:30 A.M. checking our position. Our yacht turned, but held on the Danforth anchor most of the night.

Our double size berth was in the aft cabin. When we laid down and bent our legs, our knees hit the cork ceiling. I remarked, "Oh, no. This is not going to be easy to sleep here. The way this berth is located at the opposite angle of the berths in the main cabin and forward cabin, it feels like we're being packed in a can when the yacht's tacking."

Jim replied, "We'll get used to it."

November 30th

We departed Gun Cay west of Bimini and the seas were calm. We passed the Great Bahama Bank at 1:10 P.M. Several porpoises dove across our bow. Mackie Shoal was sighted at 4 P.M. Winds started to increase. At 7:15 P.M. the winds were at 25 mph. During the night the winds increased to 35 mph and our yacht lurched constantly.

December 1st

Alan and Alicia decided to name the kitten, Trixie, after she did a somersault when the yacht heeled. Later Alan asked, Where's Trixie? We can't find her." We searched each cabin. Jim found her in the hold near the diesel engine.

We stayed over as more high winds were due tonight. A Bahamian fisherman came over in his dinghy to offer aid if necessary. "A sailboat sank further up. I'm nearby should you need help." We thanked him.

December 2nd

We left Mackie Shoal at 7:30 A.M. with very smooth seas and a sunny day to Frazier's Hog where we had difficulty setting the anchor. Alan was very helpful. We all wore wool caps and jackets in the evening. Rain pelted down and our yacht drifted. Jim was up the rest of the night as we drifted another half a mile before another anchor was set. The anchor held this time. The seas were rough and the winds howled.

December 3rd

We sailed from Fraser's Hog to Nassau in choppy seas with white caps on the waves. I asked, "What am I doing here with our two children in this terrible, scary ocean? Will we ever make it to Nassau and be able to get out on land again?" Alan was seasick.

9:30 A.M. Motored down the channel into Nassau and past the point at 10:15 A.M. At 11:00 A.M. we put our sails up and ended with a broad reach. A great sailing day ended at last after many hair-raising events.

A Sunday school lesson was shared with the children after breakfast. Every week we chose a missionary information card out of our prayer box and prayed for them.

December 8th

We took on 23.9 gallons of diesel fuel at Nassau, and also filled our fresh water tank. The produce place was government run. The oranges were sweet and as large as grapefruit. The cost was three dollars for twenty-five oranges. Good cucumbers and tomatoes were purchased. Christmas letters were written and mailed in Nassau.

Jim wrote to Dick & Mary. Spent about a week in Nassau and we'll soon be heading for the out islands. Starting to work my way south and depending on the winds should be in the Virgin Islands about mid-January. Waters here are crystal clear. Alan seems to get a little seasick, but he sure is getting tan. He's still easy to tell from the natives – he has the yellow shirt. Alicia is a great sailor. Have a Happy Holiday, Jim, Elsie, & Family plus Trixie, our cat.

December 9th

Jim's beard is well-developed and his hair has grown longer. I think he's starting to look like a pirate.

December 12th

We departed Nassau and headed to the Exumas. Countless porpoises swam on both sides of our yacht to our delight. Jim commented, "At night some porpoises look like torpedoes coming at us broadside when the moonlight is shining on them."

December 13th

We ran aground in Allan's Cay. Men from *Mistina* came over in their dinghy to assist us. When our yacht was set free, we anchored in the harbor for the night. The next morning we free-dived and discovered an exquisite coral garden on the other side of the anchorage. Jim speared his first fish with his Hawaiian sling. Alicia had taught Trixie to swim alongside of her.

Jim and I went for a swim. He pointed to the wreck of a sunken wooden trading boat not too far from our yacht. Many schools of brightly-colored fish darted around us. After we surfaced, I exclaimed, "Jim, this is so exciting and beautiful here!"

December 14th

We free-dived in Little Allan's Cay and got a large conch and some shells. A couple of cruising fellows, Greg and Bob, speared a ray. They barbecued the ray. I made date-filled cookies, four loaves of fresh bread, and onion rings. We sat around a fire and shared our food. The ray tasted good to our surprise.

December 15th

We woke up and found our yacht in an extreme careen on a sand bar in Hall's Pond. The tide had gone out during the night. The yacht tilted severely to the port side. Fresh water from our water tank had spilled into the main cabin and under the navigation table. We couldn't stand up straight. Our main cabin was a shambles.

"Dad, what happened?" Alan asked.

Jim answered, "The tide went out during the night. We'll have to wait until the tide flows back. That may take several hours though. Elsie, see what you can find for us to eat. After we crawl out onto the deck, we can sit on the edge of our portside for breakfast. It's a good time to scrub barnacles off the hull while the tide's still out."

After breakfast, we all got out into the water and scraped barnacles off the hull. About 1 P.M. the tide came back in enough to raise our yacht. We were able to straighten and clean the cabin and shove the mattress back up. Alicia sang and entertained herself.

December 17th

Our family went ashore at Norman's Cay to the trading boat. The schooner, *Walter & Mamie*, had run aground here.

December 18th

We hoisted our sails and were on our way to Warderick Wells. We then anchored near the mouth and saw one sunken rowboat. Our family went ashore and climbed to the highest point where Jim and Alan pounded a wooden stick and board to establish "MacGregor's Peak". Jim found a Portuguese fishing ball. We met Ron Pole, from Scotland, and Jane from Wisconsin on their yacht, *High Seas*.

December 21st
  I kept the children distracted from cold weather as we made fruitcake, Christmas cookies, and bread. We had to change anchorages and two anchors were set. This night Jim and I moved to the double berth in the main cabin. I woke up and my head was hot and sweaty. "Oh, no, Trixie has been sleeping on top of my hair. I yanked her off my hair and tossed her to the bottom of the berth. I wiped the perspiration off my face. "Trixie, don't climb on my head!"

December 22nd
  Our yacht arrived in Staniel Cay. We shopped at Pink Pearl, a blue store and a yellow store all up and down a one block area. We met *Convivial* here with Bob, Ginger, and her brother.

December 23rd
  We got underway from Staniel Cay and sailed to Rudder Cut. Alan vomited. We anchored for the night

December 24th
  A cold northern wind poured heavy rain on Christmas Eve day. Our yacht tossed and turned in a bay. We played Sorry, and made Christmas cards for each other. We were out of eggs. John Martin, who lived on a nearby island, motored out in his speedboat to see if we needed any help. Jim told him, "We could use some eggs."
  Mr. Martin left and returned later with a gift of eight eggs. He apologized, "I'm sorry, but I only had eight eggs."

"Jim, I never thought I'd be so grateful for eight fresh eggs. This is our Christmas gift."

December 25th
Our first Christmas on *Far Horizons* was spent at sea. We made a paper tree which the children colored with crayons. It was taped on our main cabin bulkhead. We exchanged the homemade Christmas cards that we had made for each other. Alicia's gift was a small rag doll made by an island woman. Alan got a puzzle book. We learned to be satisfied with being safe in bad weather.

December 28th
Alan went over to Tony's yacht, *Snowflake*, from Anchorage, Alaska. We heard that Dan and Sheri were having trouble near Long Island.

December 29th
9:30 A.M. Sunny and beautiful. Dan and Sheri motored into the harbor on *August Moon*. We moored out in Georgetown and did some fishing. I cooked a lovely fish dinner and we were ready to sit down to eat it when our lines got tangled up with another yacht's. Jim and I rushed topside to help untangle lines. This accomplished, we went back into the main cabin. "Oh, no, the fish is gone! Trixie, how could you?" Our cat had eaten all the pieces of fish on our plates.

December 31st
"Jim, the clothes need washing. Where can we get some fresh water?" I queried.
He answered, "I heard that there's a fresh water cistern. Let's load our dirty clothes in black plastic sacks, put these in our dinghy and motor to shore."
We did this. There we unloaded the plastic bags and carried them to the cistern. We drew up the fresh water in

buckets and scrubbed our clothes with liquid Joy. Then we rinsed them with clean fresh water from the cistern. We motored back to our yacht with wet clothes. The clothes were hung to dry on the safety rail, shrouds, or our twenty foot wooden boom. When the clothes are washed with sea water, the fabric still feels damp when dry.

"Jim, this was a wonderful opportunity," I smiled. "Yes, I miss my washer and dryer that I had back in the states. It never occurred to me that I'd have to find a cistern in a primitive area to draw fresh water up in buckets to do our laundry."

New Year's Eve was celebrated in Georgetown with our new cruising friends. New Year's Day, I was finally able to find a church. It was St. Andrews Anglican Church, and about one-hundred years old. Then our family went out to lunch at the Two Turtles. We had steamed conch. Delicious!

During the first week of January, Jim fixed the salt water tap and the fresh water tap in the galley. He changed the engine oil, and pumped twelve gallons of diesel, getting ready for our next adventure. Fresh water was put into our fresh water tank. We didn't need the bicycles, so Jim sold them. *Far Horizons* ran aground in Captain Kidd harbor. Two days later we left Georgetown on January 7th near *Interlude* with Mike and Carolyn. We hoisted out mainsail and our genoa (Charlie) as a great west wind sent us toward Jim's plotted course.

Chapter 4

Bermuda Triangle Storms

January 7th 1977

We motored out of Georgetown at 9 A.M. along with Mike and Carolyn from *Interlude*. By 10 A.M. we were over 100 fathoms of ocean. The morning was a cool 66 degrees. Jim raised the mainsail. Five hours later, the temperature had risen to 103 degrees. He decided, "It's time to set up Charlie, our large genoa." We weren't making much headway. It was a moonlit night and the seas were calm.

I remarked, "I like sailing at night when it's cooler and the children are asleep."

January 8th, 1977

4:30 P.M. We had sailed 135 miles since yesterday morning. We anchored *Far Horizons* at Atwood Harbor in beautiful Acklins Island. Jim said, "Elsie, this is a good time to mend the sails while the water is calm. I'll hold the heaviest part of the sail." I sat in the center cockpit and mended the sails and clothing with our hand-cranked sewing machine.

I replied, "This gets the job done, but I miss my electric sewing machine that I used to have in the states."

January 11th

We departed at 3 A.M. headed for Abraham Bay. 11:15 A.M. We enjoyed the porpoises that escorted us as they swam along both sides of our yacht. 3:30 P.M. Anchored at Abraham Bay, Mayaguana. Jim saw a five-foot manta ray near our yacht in the aqua water. After a wet dinghy ride, our family disembarked and pulled the dinghy to shore.

Customs was closed. We walked through backyards without fences. Men scraped scales off fish and washed the fish in large washtubs. This was a poor community with lots of children and friendly people. We passed three small churches. Women cleaned huge conch in large pots. Jim dismayed, "Can't get any propane to refill our tanks. Better go back on board." We returned to our dinghy and pushed it over the shallow water to get back to our yacht.

Our children studied their school work. Jim worked at the navigation table as he checked charts for our journey. Winds increased to 24 mph from the north by 6 P.M.

All three propane tanks were empty so we ate a cold dinner. One tank lasted a month. I said, "Jim, I'm so glad I baked four loaves of bread this morning while the ovens still had propane."

January 13th

In the morning, customs was open so they cleared our passage. I sewed a British flag out of different colors of fabric I had brought aboard. Food supplies and fresh water were loaded aboard at Abraham's Bay in Mayaguana, Bahamas.

12 Noon

We saw a seven-foot sting ray. We left Abraham's Bay for ten miles to the southern tip of Mayaguana with choppy seas and winds to 30 mph. I fixed fruit salad for dinner.

Heavy winter storms battered the area. Rough seas jolted our yacht over and over as the waves increased in size during the night. We reefed the mainsail as the driving rain attacked *Far Horizons*.

Our large table with two sitting areas on each side was dropped flat to make a double center berth in the main cabin. Jim and I moved to this center berth where the yacht was most stable. We took turns at the helm. Our duties remained the same: to be on the alert, watch out for ships, and stay on course.

Alicia fell out of her V-berth. She screamed. "Mom, Dad, I'm scared! What's wrong?"

Alan instructed her, "Alicia, hang on to the handrail so you won't get bruised. It's a bad storm." He grabbed his stomach and leaned over. "I'm sea-sick!" Alan vomited in a plastic pail.

I rushed to help the children. "Leave your life jackets on. Our yacht should ride out the storm. We'll be okay. Alan, sleep in your side berth as usual. Alicia, stay in the V- berth. Do not go outside. It's safe in here."

The waves slammed against the hull again. The wind howled, thunder boomed and lightning flashed across the sky. A huge squall forced our yacht over to her waterline, and the wind out of the sail. The yacht suffered a knockdown on her port side. More heavy rain pelted the area. The turn-buckles on the backstays had broken. The mainsail ripped horizontally and shredded at one-third of the way down. After a few minutes, our yacht righted herself. Alan breathed a sigh of relief and said, "That was too shocking!"

January 14th

Jim repaired the turnbuckles which had opened on both backstays. Jim reached inside the aft cabin from the center cockpit for the radio. He picked up the 391 beacon out of Puerto Rico, and discovered his bearing was wrong.

He contacted the Coast Guard. "Coast Guard operator, this is *Far Horizons*. This is Captain Jim MacGregor. My family aboard includes my wife, Elsie, and our two young children, Alan and Alicia. Our mainsail ripped horizontally in a severe storm and was lost overboard. We're now motoring."

Jim next notified the Cape San Juan loran station of our position. "I'm heading for Puerto Rico. Don't have enough diesel fuel to make it to the Virgin Islands."

Alan, a fast learner, listened as his dad talked to the Coast Guard. He watched how Jim handled the radio.

A Coast Guard operator returned, "Keep in touch with us. Proceed toward San Juan. You should reach San Juan by early evening." Our family shouted with relief.

Jim responded, "Thanks for your help. We've stay in contact with you." He plotted a southwest course toward San Juan.

The wind died in the evening. We motored south with our diesel engine on all night, and kept in touch with the Coast Guard. "I'll take the first watch. Sleep in the aft cabin. I'll wake you when it's your turn. Try to sleep, Elsie."

He called me after a couple of hours. "I can't see any lights. Not sure of our position. Take the helm, Elsie. I'll stay up and watch for ships."

We stayed up all night concerned for our safety and location.

The next morning, Jim used his sextant to plot our position. It had not changed. "We should have reached Puerto Rico 'cause the San Juan light should be visible twenty-eight miles out." Jim reported. He contacted the Coast Guard again.

The Coast Guard operator replied, "Puerto Rico should be forty-five miles out from where you calculated your celestial position."

I asked, "Have we been going in circles? We're forty-five miles from Puerto Rico after motoring at four to five knots all night?"

Jim sulked, "The RDF bearings must be off."

"We're still forty-five miles from San Juan two days in a row? We're further north and have to use our diesel engine to find the nearest land to repair our storm damage?" I questioned.

We ran into a worse storm. There was zero visibility and tremendous waves.

January 15th

Jim spotted a Coast Guard helicopter in the distance. We sailed all day and night. Jim and I were exhausted. He tightened the helm down so the yacht would sail itself. We both put on a safety harness in case we dozed off. One person slumped in the cockpit, the other in the aft cabin as we took turns at the helm.

We've covered 135 miles from our last anchorage and only saw two freighters.

January 17th

We ran out of cat food and were five days out from land. Trixie refused canned tuna from our supplies. I was so concerned that she wouldn't survive due to lack of food. Provision for her occurred in a most unusual way. I sat at the helm on night watch with Trixie on my lap. It was a beautiful moonlit night. I watched the sea as the reflection of the moon danced over the gentle rolling waves. I checked for other ships in the distance. Our yacht was right on course with a good wind. The rest of the family slept. "Lord, what can we feed her? I don't want her to get sick or die," I asked.

Smack! I felt a sharp blow to my right jaw. I shouted, "Ouch!" My face stung from the impact. I raised my hand to my cheek. No one was in sight. Trixie leapt off my lap into the center cockpit as her claws dug into my thighs. A flying fish flopped on the cockpit deck – dinner had arrived for Trixie. What a way to have groceries delivered!. Several more flying fish landed on our coach roof and deck. No ships were seen all night. Our family laughed together as Trixie, after she examined the strange food, went from one flying fish to another. This morning, Trixie relished her exotic feast.

January 18th

Jim paced while I rested in the berth and hoped for the storm to subside. He said, "I'm going out to check the damage. Stay in the cabin, Elsie."

The yacht jerked violently to the starboard side. I was thrown out of the center berth. "Help, Jim! I can't move. My leg is trapped. The table top . . ." I tried to get free. I couldn't budge the heavy table top.

Jim turned back into the main cabin. He lifted the heavy table top to free my leg. I was then able to stand. He put on a safety harness, and struggled naked out of the hatch in the downpour. I gasped as I watched him out of the porthole. I clutched my fingers on the safety rail in the main cabin. Jim lost his balance and fell. *Far Horizons* continued to be pounded from the heavy erratic waves. I yelled, "Jim, are you okay? Hang on." I shuddered. What would happen to the children and me if Jim got swept overboard?

Jim got up and struggled along the coach roof to check the shrouds in the driving rain. The backstays and the shroud on the starboard side were loose.

I pleaded, "Lord Jesus, I can't bear another night in these storms. Please clear the pathway for us on top of the water as you opened the sea for the Israelites so many years ago. Every time I take the helm, I tell the waves to hold their peace. I choose to trust you, Lord."

The storm had ceased by early morning. Glistening rays of sunlight danced off the surface of the silver water. The glare off the ocean surface appeared surreal. The surface of the water looked glazed. No land was in sight. No other ships and no planes were seen. An eerie stillness hovered over our yacht. An unpredictable and deceiving ocean loomed before us.

There wasn't hot food or a warm beverage for six days. We missed the coffee to keep us awake. We motored two more days with the same heading and no progress. There wasn't a cloud in the sky.

Alan said, "Mom, Dad, what was that noise? I heard a loud booming sound."

Jim and I looked at him and agreed that we hadn't heard anything. Jim got the shotgun out. He searched the sky again. No planes were visible. We scanned the horizon. Still no land and no other boats were in sight.

Several minutes later, Jim and I heard a large group of distorted voices that chanted in muffled tones high in the sky. The sound of these eerie voices moved closer. The voices erupted in a discordant discussion. We could only hear the sound of voices. Nothing was visible in any direction.

Jim shouted, "Elsie, pray!"

I gasped, "Father, please protect us. Lord Jesus, I claim your authority and I bind Satan and the evil forces above us. They have no power over us in Jesus' Name. Thank you for protecting our family and our yacht."

Our yacht alone on this eerie sea appeared to be a target. The invisible voices passed overhead and faded off into the distance.

I asked, "Jim, did you hear them?"

Jim breathed a sigh of relief and said, "Yes, it terrified me."

Twenty minutes later, we heard the weird sounds of unnatural voices as they came back from the direction they had gone. I pleaded, "Christ Jesus, you are our protection. Save us." The eerie voices got closer. We sensed impending danger. We held our breath. Unseen forces moved over our yacht and left. Our family breathed sighs of relief and thanked God for sparing us and our home, *Far Horizons*.

Mammoth ground swells developed in the sea. They appeared as large hills and valleys that our yacht had to climb. Winds and black clouds continued to form. Jim and I slumped in the cockpit. Both of us were drained of energy.

Jim's solution, "We've been driving ourselves too hard, staying up night and day. Let's take turns every hour and drink some water."

The yacht climbed up the side of one mountainous wave and fell down the other side. Wave after wave continued. Jim reflected, "Only one other time did I see an ocean like this . . . when I had been in the Navy for almost four years. The battleship, *Wisconsin*, was anchored about eight miles out from Mexico. We tried to launch forty-foot liberty boats. The ship rolled from side-to-side."

"What happened? Did any liberty boats get launched?" I asked.

"We couldn't do it. The liberty boat would catch the top of the sea. Then the sea would drop off forty-fifty feet down. The sailors would let off the lines; and bang, the sea would come up. There was too much line. They'd pull in line; the sea would go back up. The sea would drop out again."

Jim studied the charts as he looked for a harbor. The emergency kit, safety harnesses, flare gun and flares stood ready. He came out of the main cabin while I stayed at the helm. Screeching winds and a pitch black night increased the terror.

Jim appeared confused. He decided. "Let's get to a harbor to repair storm damage. I think Fajardo, Puerto Rico is southwest of San Juan."

Another rough squall crashed across the sea. We fought to keep our heading. I tried to bend my fingers. My hands were stiff as I held the helm against the force of the waves. A heavy downpour battered the area.

Alan relayed over the radio, "Mayday, mayday. This is *Far Horizons*. Can anyone hear me?"

No answer. Alan took a deep breath, leaned his head back, sighed and tried again. "Mayday, mayday, this is *Far Horizons*." He waited for a reply.

A voice came over the radio. "I hear you, *Far Horizons*. I'm sending your message to the Coast Guard. This is a U.S. naval radio operator. They weren't picking your message up. They'll send out two Navy helicopters from Roosevelt Roads Naval Base."

Alan whooped with joy. "Spirit Sam, Spirit Sam. Thank you for contacting us. We'll shoot off flares as we spot your helicopters."

A Canadian helicopter that was visiting Roosevelt Roads U.S. Naval Base flew out to search for us. A Coast Guard helicopter was also dispatched. Jim loaded the flare gun and fired off ten to twelve flares into the sky. The helicopters avoided the storm. They didn't see the flares.

I labored to hold the helm in the storm as the yacht cut into huge waves. My hands hurt from grasping the helm for so long. I whispered a prayer while I questioned my faith. "When I'm afraid, I'll continue to trust in you. Save us, Lord."

Will we live through this? We have to keep going to reach a safe harbor. This is obedience? This is faith? This is terror! My thoughts raced.

A shoreline with trees appeared at dusk. Jim admitted he no longer had control as he took over the helm. He directed *Far Horizons* toward a point. "That must be Puerto Rico. Where is the harbor?" A lighthouse and a flashing buoy appeared.

Darkness covered the sky. Enormous black clouds shot forth from the Puerto Rican rain forest. A squall hit. Gigantic waves exploded over the yacht. Zero visibility. Unmarked reefs. VHF was out of range.

Jim tuned into AM frequency. "Mayday, mayday, this is *Far Horizons*. Coast Guard, we've lost all directional bearing. Two fathoms at a crack."

Jim steered *Far Horizons* in line between the one flashing buoy and a lighthouse on a hill. Where was the harbor? We motored up to the buoy. Three to four fathoms, then toward the lighthouse. Then five to six fathoms. Two fathoms! *Far Horizons* fell off and Jim circled the yacht around.

He yelled, "West is land, east the reefs. We're trapped between them!" Jim laid our yacht over on its side and gave fuel power as he heard surf and saw trees.

Double red lights flashed on and off from the shore signaling danger. "There must be a reef. What does the fathometer read?"

I shouted, "Two fathoms! Now it reads three to four fathoms, five to six fathoms. Two fathoms again! We're in danger!"

"Elsie, take over the helm. I'll check the chart again. Turn and go out to sea!"

Far Horizons rolled from side-to-side. I spun the helm to turn back into deeper water. The yacht laid over on its side, spun 180 degrees, and out to sea. *Far Horizons* surfed down the front of the gigantic waves. I had lost control of our yacht. I commanded, "Satan, I bind you from destroying our yacht or harming our family in Jesus' mighty Name. We are protected by your shed blood, Jesus."

Alan relayed back on the radio with the Navy operator. "Two helicopters came near the edge of the storm. They didn't see us. My dad's firing off more flares."

"I hear you, *Far Horizons*. We're searching for you. Stay in contact with us."

Winds screamed at 65 miles an hour. I saw a third helicopter as it circled in the distance. Alan broadcasted, "Spirit Sam, we're not abandoning ship. Find us, and lead us to a safe harbor." Alan called out different bearings as Jim gave them to our son to relay to the Navy operator.

"Alan, tell him that the lighthouse is thirty degrees to our yacht. The water depth is three and a half fathoms. We're heading north. Firing two flares now."

"Spirit Sam, my dad says lighthouse thirty degrees from us, water depth three and a half fathoms. We're heading north. He's firing two flares. Do you see them?"

There was static on the radio frequency. Alan tried again, "I can't read you. Repeat . . . do you see our flares?" No answer. There was more static.

Little Alicia sat on the galley floor as her arms hugged her life jacket. She prayed, "I'm scared. I don't know what to do. Are we going to die? Jesus, help us."

Two middle-aged fishermen who knew the area motored out in their Boston Whaler to help our crippled yacht. Jim heard their motor. One fisherman shouted, "Ahoy there! We heard your lad on the radio. You're between two reefs! We'll guide you into Fajardo. Follow us."

Jim exclaimed, "What are you doing out here on a night like this?"

The fishermen joked, "We're out from Villa Marina and we're looking for business." The fishermen climbed aboard *Far Horizons* and tied their Boston Whaler behind our yacht. They guided us between the two reefs into the harbor. Our battered yacht limped into the marina and we tied up at the dock. Our family thanked the fishermen, Larry Abel and Gary Ahrens. The first hot meal in six days welcomed us at the Fajardo Marina that night. Our yacht was a disaster.

January 21st

Customs cleared us at 1:00 P.M. All our clothing was soaked with sea water. But we had the use of a laundromat at last! Cold fresh water, but it beats washing at a cistern or washing clothes with sea water. Alicia's cabin was a mess.

Both V-berth storage units were full of sea water. Salt water was under the galley cupboard and sink. A peanut butter jar was broken.

I shuddered from exhaustion. My hands seemed frozen. I couldn't straighten my fingers. We rested for two days. All clothes and bedding were washed in fresh water to get the dampness of the seawater out. The bilge had three inches of seawater in it.

Jim said, "Elsie, it's going to take several days to dry out the flooring, and to clean up our yacht. Things are strewn in a mess."

An islander in his thirties reported some of the damage. "You've been in the southern part of the Bermuda Triangle. Navy ships have had their instruments either quit working or spin crazily. Some planes have been mysteriously lost. Glad you made it in this part of the ocean."

Alone back on board, I jerked at my hair before I collapsed to my knees. I pleaded with the Lord. "I'm like shattered glass . . . in dozens of pieces." My body shook with exhaustion and fear. "Lord, there isn't any way that I have the strength to sail anymore. Lord, you have to put the pieces together . . . I can't." I blew my nose several times and wiped my tears. "I love Jim, but why do I have to be the one to give in? They must've been romantic delusions. It hurts when he ignores me."

Chief Mike Taylor, an officer at the Roosevelt Roads Naval Base, had listened to Alan's radio transmission. He told him, "Alan, you're a hero. My 13 year old son couldn't have done as good a job as you did and you're only eight! Alan, you're a brave boy. I'm going to give you and your family a tour of the naval base."

Our family was invited to the Taylor home for dinner. Ruth Taylor, a brown-haired navy wife, showed us a heading in the local newspaper: WAVES MENACE WEST COAST AS WEATHER SOURS. The article continued: Winds sixty-five miles an hour, high seas fifty feet. One boat on radar screen disappeared. Severe flooding reported in area. A container ship lost twenty-nine containers overboard.

"Our diesel engine ran thirty-six hours without interruption. If it had failed, then we had ninety feet of chain and our CQR anchor. If that didn't catch . . ." Jim's voice drifted. He gulped as he turned away in silence.

Mike Taylor insisted, "Alan was the hero."

The following day, after meeting other cruising families, Jim and the kids came back aboard *Far Horizons*. One sailor played his guitar for us. He sang, "Oh, sing me laddies . . . of the fine lassies."

Jim dropped another verbal plan. "We'll stay here a few more days, before we head for the Virgin Islands. Let's stock up on supplies here and fill our tank with fresh water. I've decided it's best to sail for Europe first."

I flinched in fear and turned my head away from Jim. *It's impossible for me to go sailing again. I'm still in shock.*

January 23rd

Alicia and I took a publico into town on Sunday and visited a church associated with a local Bible bookstore. I was delighted to meet Reverend C. Anderson and his wife, Margaret. They were from Grace Evangelical Church in Fajardo. He asked, "Would you give your testimony of how the Lord helped you through all the storms at my church?"

I agreed, "Yes, I'll need a ride to the church." The next Sunday morning I took a deep breath before I stepped into their car. This was the first church yielded to God that I attended since the first part of last November. During the service, they had a Spanish interpreter for me. With the Lord's help, I was able to relate the events which I'd been trying to forget. If I didn't have the Lord's strength and courage, I'd be a basket case.

February 6th

Mrs. Marion Rexford came aboard to visit and wrote in our guest log: God is thy refuge and strength, a very present help in trouble.

I wrote in my journal: We've lived on our yacht six months today.

February 7th

Our fresh water tank was emptied, cleaned and refilled. I went to the evening church service with Margaret Anderson. It was a wonderful service. I felt a refreshing as I heard the word of God.

February 8th

Alan and Alicia ran down the Fajardo Marina dock with their fishing poles. Several children joined them. Alicia caught a huge green coiled object. She dropped the rod on the dock. She barreled back to *Far Horizons*. She yelled, "Mom, Dad, I caught a green pumpkin! Come and see it!"

I stepped onto the dock with a questioning look. At that moment, Alicia tripped and fell overboard into deep water. I yelled, "Help! My little daughter stumbled on the dock! She's disappeared below water! Help! Someone please help!" She sank and couldn't be seen. Jim dove in after her. Alan handed Alicia a long-handed fishing net to grasp when she surfaced. I pulled her up by the hand. Jim gave her a push up onto the dock. I hugged her, "Alicia, Alicia. Are you okay?"

Alicia pushed back her red hair, wiped her freckled face, and caught her breath. "I'm okay. Hurry! Let's go, I want you to see my green pumpkin." We walked around the corner of the dock. A huge, green Moray eel was wrapped around Alicia's fishing pole. Several people were shocked to see such a large Moray eel.

I warned, "Alicia, Alan. Don't touch it! It may bite you. Jim, can you get that eel off her fishing pole?"

Jim attempted to dislodge the two foot Moray eel as he poked it with a long stick. "Stand back, everyone. These eels can bite." Adults and children backed away as they watched Jim. After a few attempts, he detached the eel and tossed it back in the water.

I declared, "Enough fishing. Alicia, back to the yacht, wash up and change into dry clothes." I followed behind her. *At least we weren't out at sea this time.*

Fajardo is a beautiful area with mountains and lush greenery. Jim says, "Elsie, this is a provisional stop. We're going to the West Indies next." He remained determined to have his quest fulfilled.

My marriage vow to my husband "for better or worse" demanded more sacrifices. I was still in shock. *I can't get back on board. I'm trapped!*

Chapter 5

Cruising Adjustments

"Jim, please hold the sail steady while I turn the crank handle on this sewing machine." A heavy needle with strong thread joined the torn edges of our sail. I sighed, "This would have been so much easier with an electric sewing machine. Well, this is better than having to stitch it by hand. I hope this holds the sail together until our new mainsail is ready." I finished the mending job.

Jim announced, "The direction of the winds decides where we sail. I've ordered an Aries wind vane to make sailing a lot easier. We've done a lot of beating into the wind."

"What a relief. That will help us a lot."

The sea was calm. Jim said, "Can't send the kids out to play, there are sharks in the ocean. Time for their school lessons since the weather is good."

I directed, "Children, get out your phonics workbooks. Dad will help you with math later." Alan and Alicia got their workbooks out of the locker and turned to the day's assignment.

The uncertainty of daily life started to be as frightening as Jim's appearance. He began to increase his drinking of wine and beer. He looked like a cave man. What has changed my husband into this stranger? This wasn't the man I married. He was an industrial engineer, next a real estate salesman. Then he became a real estate broker. He craved being at sea so he dropped all normal means of living and now risked our lives.

February 9th

"Ahoy, do you have any books to trade?" Jim shouted. Another yacht was anchored in the harbor. Swapping books became an important checkpoint when we were in a harbor. This was a great way to meet new people. Our children also learned to exchange books with other cruising kids.

"Sure, come on over and bring some of your books. I'll see if I've read them." So, Jim got in our dinghy and motored over to the other yacht. We might only see people for a few hours or perhaps a day before they left for their various destinations.

Jim wrote to our friends, Mary and Dick Wilson: Better mark any mail that you send to us "Hold for Arrival". The mail sometimes took several months to get to us at the different islands.

When the weather was calm, I wrote notes in my journal. I missed hearing from friends and family. I hoped that they kept us in their prayers.

"The clouds are dark, there's a rain shower coming," I said. "It's time to get a fresh water bath." It felt so good to let the rain water cleanse our skin from the salt water. Alicia and I stood near the bow in our bathing suits. I scrubbed her first with soap, and then rinsed her hair. Jim and Alan took their rain showers next.

February 11th

In the evening we saw lights off the Virgin Islands. I remarked, "The lights look like jewels on a ring. They're beautiful."

Jim pointed, "Pay attention to that star shell fired over Culebra by the Navy!" There were a lot of yachts anchored in this calm harbor.

February 13th

We left Culebra at 7 A.M. and anchored down in Charlotte Amalie, St. Thomas at 12:30 P.M. The next day we took our mainsail (with a two yards long rip in it) to a sail maker for repair. The shop was closed. He got married today.

February 19th 1977

I wrote to Mary and Dick Wilson. Finally received your Christmas card yesterday! Cute! Another letter post-marked November 10th found us. Anchored in Charlotte Amalie Harbor in San Thomas, Virgin Islands as we want to test our mainsail out (it's fixed). We'll sail to St Croix for four to five days, then return here and have reefing points put in. We should be here the next couple of weeks. Next address for approximately one and a half months: Captain Jim MacGregor "Far Horizons" Lord Nelson Yacht Harbor in Antigua, West Indies. Love, Elsie

February 24th

6:41 A.M. Alicia had her first experience of being seasick while on the sail to Christensted, St. Croix. Our new friends, Ron and Jane, sailed the same passage on their yacht, *High Seas*. We arrived at 3:30 P.M. and docked.

Ron asked, "Jim, would you go over the charts for the Atlantic crossing? Which route are you taking?" The sea captains poured over the navigation routes.

March 3rd

Alan retrieved a man's lenses and retrieved another man's dinghy. Alan reported, "Trixie has fleas." Shopping was not as easy as in the states. Four days later, we bought a cat's flea collar to put on Trixie.

March 25th

Jim allowed Alicia to steer part of the way to the East end of Tortola. There were large ocean swells on the trip to Virgin Gorda. We anchored near Mosquito Island in Virgin Gorda Sound. The children and I snorkeled while Jim dove with his scuba gear on to clean the hull. Alan said, "Mom, did you see that large turtle on the ocean floor?" I nodded and smiled.

March 29th

We hauled *Far Horizons* out at Bird's Creek in Virgin Gorda. A new zinc plate coating was applied to the keel. We painted the hull white with a blue stripe and finished at 6:30 P.M. Alan smacked at the mosquitoes, "This name was right on, but at least we had a cool breeze to work in so the paint will dry faster."

March 30th

Back in the water and over to Bitter End where we anchored. Our family went ashore. Alicia held out her little hand. "These are the most fascinating tiny birds. Four of them are eating sugar out of my hand at the same time. What are they called?"

Alan answered, "I was told that they are called Banana Quits because of their yellow-colored feathers on their chests."

Jim speared a large lobster and gathered three large conchs. I made lobster salad sandwiches. Jim and I played cribbage. He was ahead eighteen games. I reminded him,

"Remember when I was ahead and you got angry and knifed the cribbage board?" He glared.

April 5th

We left Bitter End at 5:30 P.M. with choppy seas and high winds. It was a rough and wet voyage. Jim helmed the entire way until 4:40 P.M. the next day. Alan and Alicia were seasick and vomited. I was seasick for the first time and also regurgitated. A heavy thunderstorm chased us before we were able to anchor in a turbulent harbor at St. Eustatius.

April 6th

Jim ordered, "Alan, I need you to climb the mast and untangle that line."

I countered, "Oh, no. The waves in this harbor are too violent. It's dangerous for our son!" The mast was forty-six feet high. With our yacht pitching from side-to-side this was criminal.

Alan complied, "Okay, dad, tell me what to do."

"Lord Jesus, keep him safe," I pleaded. The mast swayed violently back and forth from the rough waters. Alan climbed up the tall mast.

Alicia called, "Mom, where's Alan?"

I ordered, "Alicia, stay down in the cabin. Your brother is up at the top of the mast. Do not come out for anything!"

Alan got the line untangled. He held on tightly and came down safely.

We left St. Eustatius at 9:30 A.M. and headed toward St. Barts. The seas were moderately high. We ran into fierce winds when we rounded a point. The toe rail was in sea water within a few minutes when our sails back winded. The gusts blew across from the mountains. Jim hollered, "Elsie, we'll have to reef the main." This worked well after he locked the helm.

St. Barts was charming. There were various cruising yachts in the harbor. I suggested, "There's a French bakery. Let's get fresh bread and pastries." We started to explore the island with its white sand beaches.

Jim said, "We need to find some foul weather gear before we leave the West Indies."

I asked, "Why didn't you get us these in the states?"

His response, "I thought it would be cheaper here."

April 13th

We bought twenty-one grapefruits and a stalk of bananas from a native on a Dominican boat for only three dollars.

April 14th

Our family took a bus to the French town of Marigot. The majority of the roofs were corrugated tin sheets. Heavy winds and rain hit us at three in the morning. Alan returned a crate for a boat. They gave him ten bananas and four coconuts for returning the crate.

April 16th

We motored past St. Christopher (St. Kitts), a beautiful green island with mountains. Jim and Alan anchored *Far Horizons* at Charleston, Nevis. This was another lovely island with the shoreline lined with lots of palm trees and beach. There were donkeys, pigs, and goats on the roads. Alan shouted, "I met a native boy in Nevis who still believes in dragons!"

April 17thb

I attended a very old Methodist church. I passed by an old black woman sitting in a pew. She looked up at me and held out her hand. "My husband beats me. He poked a stick in my eye." Her left eye was missing and indented.

I prayed, "Lord, please comfort her and protect her from any more beatings. Encourage this special woman. Thank you."

The women and girl children wore knee-length dresses. They did not wear slacks or shorts.

Alan gushed, "I love sugar cane! It's so sweet." He enjoyed diving off the wharf with the native boys. It was a sunny day.

There were numerous native trading boats with very long booms in the harbor. They were in competition for selling fruits and vegetables. We bought two-thirds of a stalk of bananas for sixty cents.

April 19th

We sailed using our genoa and mainsail with an east wind following to Montserrat. A whale was sighted between Pinnacle Rock and Montserrat. Alan read the entire book *Pete and Penny* (about thinking and thanking). Alicia was able to read Dr. Seuss's *The Foot Book* by herself.

April 20th

The jib and mainsail were reefed on the trip to Antigua. We arrived at 6 P.M. and found English Harbor with a nice beach, a thatched hut and enclosed houses with pretty flowers. The harbor was calm with cruising yachts and charter boats. Our family went over to Admiral's Inn for dinner.

April 21st

Jim was asked to be a pirate in a film *So the Story Goes*. He already looks the part with his scraggly beard and long, messy hair. This was for a Canadian television series. This film was about Mary Read and Anne Bonny – two of the most famous and treacherous lady pirates. They were both convicted of piracy during the eighteenth century. They disguised themselves as men. The narrator was Austin Wills.

They filmed on location ashore and on the pirate ship. Jim boasted, "My part as a pirate includes the scene where my wench grabs my pistol and then I stick my finger down the barrel. There's also a part on the pirate ship where a redcoat forces me back when I was ready to run him through with my sword. It's fun. I got to holler as I'm being thrown overboard from the rail of the ship." He grimaced and waved his arms.

May 8th
 The children and I visited the Galilean Baptist Church in Antigua where I gave my testimony.
 Jim explained, "We'll be leaving for Bermuda in three days. We can't take Trixie to England with us because there is six month quarantine for animals."
 Alicia cried, "I don't want to lose Trixie. I need her. She's my kitty. I love her."
 The Captain rules, so Trixie was given to a worker at the local Marina.

May 9th
 Jim met a British sailor, Hugh Wilcoxson, who was in the royal Navy for over twenty years and was now retired. He had a smaller sailboat, *Dowa*. He asked, "Jim, I don't want to sail my boat across the Atlantic. I'm from Selby Yorkshire, England. I'd like to hitch a ride with you. I'll crew for you. I need to get to Portsmouth, England. I'll leave mine in Antigua."
 Jim rubbed his bearded chin, "Hmm, that would help. We're going to Bermuda first. Get your gear aboard and come for dinner tonight."
 He explained, "Elsie, he'll take watches to make this first ocean crossing easier for you."

May 11th 1977

On our twenty-first wedding anniversary, *Far Horizons* left Antigua and headed north toward Bermuda with a stranger aboard as a crew member. "Jim, our wind vane is working great," I approved. Alan gave me a picture of a zebra for our anniversary gift. I put it in the head. We really are a zoo living on the ocean.

May 16th

We traveled 551 miles in the last five days. We were forced to change course last night when Jim spotted a cargo ship at the same time and place we were headed.

May 17th

"Alicia, today is your sixth birthday! We're having balloons, cake and presents for you." We sang "Happy Birthday" to Alicia.

She opened her presents. "Thanks for the puzzles and coloring book.. Oh, I like these jelly beans. Want some jelly beans, Alan?"

May 18th

This was our eighth full day at sea. It was necessary to use the diesel motor due to no wind. Alan reported a ketch aft. The ocean looked glassy. I fixed canned chicken and fresh dumplings for dinner. Jim decided, "This was a very good crossing. This is easier with a wind vane and with Hugh helping."

Alan finished his Score reading program!

11:10 P.M. Hugh wondered, "There's a ship very close to us. It's making strange maneuvers. It may be military." Jim changed our course. Then he fired a flare as the ship came right toward us.

Venus shone bright in the morning on the horizon when a tanker was sighted.

Chapter 6

North Atlantic Crossing

J im came up with a new plan. He said, "I have a new idea. Why don't we give each person one hour by themselves in the aft cabin? Then after that hour, another person gets their turn."

The kids and I bounced up and down. We yelled in unison, "Yes, yes, yes!"

Alan suggested, "If it's stormy, someone can crawl through the engine and storage area and slip into the aft cabin with a book. Then you still get your one hour of privacy!"

The family agreed and gave me the first hour. I said, "Boy, do I need privacy. See you in an hour." I left for the aft cabin with my journal and another book. Ah, to be alone at last. What a luxury!

After I finished resting in the aft cabin, I sat out in the cockpit when I overheard Jim and Alan get into an important discussion. Alan complained, "I miss school. I wish we were back in California."

Jim asked, "Why? Don't you like sailing?"

Alan answered, "Sailing's okay. Sometimes it gets boring. Especially if there isn't any wind." He took a deep breath and confessed, "The reason I want to go back to California is, I won't have to be cooped up in this floating zoo any longer."

Jim retorted, "And you're the chief animal."

Letter to Marilyn: The carpet sank last week. We put our galley carpet out to dry on the coach roof. The wind picked it up and tossed it overboard. We shower on deck using our new large weed killer spray can that we fill with fresh water. This is saving fresh water. We have learned to look for rain clouds so we could take a fresh water shower. Otherwise we dive in the sea unless we're underway. Your letters are a blessing to me! I thank the Lord for our precious friendship. I can really see how the Lord used all events to prepare us for what lies ahead. Thank you for all your prayers and letters. Love, Elsie

May 20th 1977

Alan met several local Bermuda boys who taught him how to play cricket. They used a red leather ball and a flat wooden bat. He loved having friends. They shared stories and played games on land.

May 23rd

Butane tank filled. Preparations for our North Atlantic crossing were completed.

May 24th

Alan's ninth birthday is today. He went ashore in Bermuda and played cricket with three island boys. His curly brown hair blew in the wind. He laughed as he chased after the ball. I baked a birthday cake for Alan. Alicia helped to set the table with plastic forks, paper plates, and paper napkins. After the cake was cooling, I placed it on the table.

Alicia said, "Mom, let me count the candles. I see one, two, three, four, five, six, seven, eight, and nine. I want to blow up the balloons too."

I agreed. "Okay. Alicia, I'll tie the knot on the end of the balloons, and put a ribbon on the end." I lit the candles, left the galley and called to Alan from the cockpit. "Alan, bring your friends and come aboard for a treat."

Sheldon Steele, Antoine Daniels, and Robert Minks climbed aboard. Alan peeked into the main cabin and grinned when he saw his birthday cake and party decorations. He exclaimed, "Even balloons! I'm glad that I have new friends to celebrate with me.

Thanks, Mom and Dad. Alicia, did you help Mom with my party?"

Alicia grinned, "Mom made me help."

We all sang "Happy Birthday" to Alan. He said, "This is my best birthday, to have friends and to be able to play cricket today." He opened a homemade birthday card from us. There was a ten dollar bill in it. He closed his eyes as he relished the moment.

May 25th

1:00 P.M. We left Bermuda with sunny skies. It was a good sailing day. A weather reporter stated, "Beautiful weather the next six days."

May 26th

It started raining about 2:30 P.M. The winds increased and the sea waves kept building, we reefed our mainsail. Jim said, "Alicia could sleep through a hurricane." During the night, we had to reef the mainsail even lower. Jim griped, "We're getting clobbered and tossed around like a ping pong ball." From then on it was a miserable trip. Rain, too much wind, no wind, more rain, and then the wind came from the wrong direction.

A storm ripped the jib, bent the stanchion, and the port shroud was broken. I banged my head and shoulder on the boom vang. I was thrown into the aft cabin.

"Jim, help!" He pulled me out of the cabin. We dropped the mainsail and the jib. We rode out the worst part of the storm until the late afternoon.

Jim muttered, "If it's like this, no one would own a boat."

Alan overheard his dad. "Are we going back to California?"

Jim rebutted, "No!"

May 27th

Our family woke up. Jim pointed, "Check out the pack of pilot whales following us. There must be about thirty of them." This was disturbing. The pilot whales followed closely behind our yacht for an hour. The winds and storm eased enough to enable us to raise the storm jib and get control over the direction of our compass heading. I exclaimed, "Thank You, Lord!"

May 28th Saturday

The alfalfa was started. The eggs were turned (necessary to do every three days without a refrigerator). Captain Jim said, "It's a good day for the children to do their school lessons."

It rained all night. Some progress was made after we hoisted the Genoa, a large foresail which we named "Charlie."

May 30th

I rejoiced, "Sun! At last! Let's hang out clothes and bedding out to dry." Jim spotted a 50 foot gray sperm whale at 2:00 P.M. about 100 feet from the port side of our yacht. It was too close to us. Jim pointed to the whale and put his forefinger in front of his lips. He warned, "Look! Be quiet.

Don't make any noise or it might think we're a playmate. I don't want it to bump us." Our family watched the whale for several minutes. It made a large circle around our yacht. Then the whale disappeared.

Alan asked, "Where did the whale go? I hope it's not underneath us." No one could see it. Suddenly, we heard the stream of air and water shoot forth from the whale's spout on the starboard side. We turned and held our breath. Now it was only a few feet off from our yacht. This was a special day to remember this curious visitor.

June 1st

Alicia lost her second tooth – lower, right center. I made a salad with the alfalfa and mung beans (our only salad ingredients available). The salad was a rare treat.

Eight ships and a tanker were sighted during the night. Our wind vane was not working. Alan was seasick. Jim was not able to use his sextant to check our position due to an overcast sky.

June 3rd

Our passenger, Hugh, opened his sea bag and took out part of his gear. He commented, "This is my crossbow. It's been reliable for fishing or protection." He had not shown us this weapon until we were well on our way.

I asked, "Jim, did you know that Hugh had brought this weapon aboard before we left Antigua?"

Jim shook his head, "No."

June 4th

I was on watch on a sunny clear day and checked all directions for commercial vessels. There was a light breeze. Dolphins were dancing in the sea ahead of our bow. They were so beautiful to watch. Both the mainsail and Genoa were up. We were making good headway. I need to bake fresh bread today while it's still good weather. I miss my family and friends back in the states. Alan and Alicia need some children to play with and they need to get fresh milk. They are both so brave.

I asked Jim, "I've been thinking. How do you call a family home when you live on a yacht? I got this idea to make a family flag out of this yellow and red plaid fabric. What do you think?"

He replied, "Great idea. Do it." Jim took over the helm.

I measured and cut the plaid fabric. Next, I sewed a French seam on the edges with my hand cranked sewing machine. I made a fold on one side for a rope to slide through. The ends were secured to hold the rope. I held up the flag and smiled. "Now there's a way to tie it to the starboard shroud. I'm done. How does it look?"

Captain Jim instructed, "Great. Okay, kids. Should there be trouble aboard when one of us is ashore, hoist our family flag from the starboard shroud. It's large enough to be seen from shore."

Alan agreed, "Okay, Dad. Mom, that's a great idea. Thanks for taking good care of us. Why is our American flag the only flag flown from the stern?"

Jim explained, "The flag flown from the stern shows what country the yacht is registered in."

Alan pressed, "Countries we visit . . . where do their flags fly from?"

Jim said, "From the starboard shroud." Alan nodded his head.

The wind picked up. Jim adjusted the sails. I was at the helm. The children squirmed. Jim suggested, "We're about halfway across the Atlantic Ocean, so let's have a party."

I called, "I've made the Halfway Cake to celebrate today. Your dad and I have presents for you, Alicia and Alan." I brought out small gift packages.

Alicia opened her packages and held up new crayons and a coloring book. She said, "Oh, good, it's about schools of fish, seahorses and porpoises. Thanks. Alan, what did you get?"

Alan slid open the tape on his package. He pulled out a pair of swim fins, and tried on a new face mask with a snorkel. He grinned. "Great. Thanks, I can hardly wait to try these out."

Jim spoke, "You're welcome. Keep up the good work. Our next landfall will be the city of Horta in the Azores Islands."

Ten days later, we tied up to the main harbor wall in Horta. Painted on the wall were the names and dates of many yachts that crossed the Atlantic Ocean to the Azores. The next day Alan painted a picture of Far Horizons on the harbor wall at Horta. He painted June 16th, the words "Far Horizons" and 21 days for the crossing. I asked, "Alan, move to the right. Hold still." I snapped his picture as he stood proudly alongside of his memorable artwork.

Jim said, "Great job, son." He patted Alan on the shoulder.

Our family walked into Horta. Black and white sidewalks in different patterns decorated the city. Women wore black hosiery, black shoes, black scarves, black dresses, and black coats as they walked in the town.

Alicia asked, "Look at the ladies. Why are they all wearing black?"

I told her, "It must be the custom for all of them to wear black."

Jim commented, "The men hunt whales with harpoons . . . the old-fashioned way. They're called "whalers.""

Alan perked up, "Awesome. I'd like to talk with a whaler, and go out in his whaling boat."

Mrs. Rigazo offered, "My husband said to let you use our washtubs to wash your clothes in fresh water. Our washtubs are in our backyard. Do you have enough soap?" She stood short, plump, and happy-faced with black hair.

We took our dirty clothes over to her backyard and washed the seawater out of them. I told her, "Thank you for the use of your washtubs and the fresh water. We'll take the clean clothes back to our yacht to dry out."

She said, "It's okay. I'm glad to help your family."

We strung the clean, wet clothes over the safety rail and shrouds to dry. A stranger walked up to us and said, "Is this the laundry boat?"

I replied, "You got it, mister."

Isaiah 40:29 KJV *"He giveth power to the faint; and to them that have no might he increaseth strength."*

Our yacht is our only home. We had weathered many storms (both spiritual and natural). My daughter started to sing a song that ministered to my heart. She didn't know that I could hear her.

She sang, "Oh, can it be. Oh, dear Lord, I have found the secret to know you. Lord, you are so good to me. You've given me the strength I needed to cross the Atlantic, and you have more strength than I need. I am weak but you are strong. You came to the earth and died on the cross for our sins. You can give me, O Lord, what I need to get back to America. Thank you."

My eyes filled with tears and the tears ran down my cheeks. I prayed, "Thank You, Jesus for allowing me to hear such faith flowing from the heart of this blue water little sailor."

Her official crew position was: "Cookie, fender tender". Her job was to put the rubber white fenders between the yacht and the dock when we'd come into port to protect the hull. To have heard how God had strengthened this child was overwhelming. "Thank You, Lord, for the privilege of witnessing your divine power at work in my little girl." As she sang, I was also strengthened.

Our garden at sea was kept on the galley floor inside a small locker. Alfalfa sprouts and mung beans (a type of bean sprouts) grew in separate glass jars. Cheesecloth, secured by rubber bands, covered the mouth of the jars. I directed, "Alicia, pour fresh water into the jars of the alfalfa sprouts and mung beans. Next, pour it out through the cheesecloth."

"Mom, these taste so good. I like the crunchy sound." She removed the jars from the locker, rinsed the vegetables, and drained the fresh water out. She put the jars back and finished her job. "See, Mom, I can do it." She smiled as she dried her hands.

Fellow yachtsmen brought us to a sixteenth century fort. A formal dinner was served by waiters who wore dress trousers and long-sleeved jackets. A white napkin was draped over their arms as they waited on their customers. The fort was built with large gray stone blocks.

I gasped, "Nine pieces of silverware each? We each have three goblets? And we're in cruising clothes. I feel out of place." This seemed unreal.

Jim smiled, "Cream of carrot soup. Delicious. Mmm. First main course . . . fish with potatoes."

Alan added, "Second course . . . chicken with a different style potatoes. I'm stuffed."

Alicia hummed, "Carrots . . . cake. I feel like a princess. Is this a dream?"

Jim commented, "This is very reasonable. Hard to believe, it's less than what we'd pay for a lunch in the States. It's only four dollars each. Enjoy because we leave for Ireland in the morning."

Chapter 7

Landfall In Ireland

June 23rd 1977

We met Goaliahu Shtirner, the first Israelite to circumnavigate single-handed on *New Penny*. He was tall and thin with a full black beard. "It must have been difficult to keep watch 24 hours a day," I said. He invited us aboard. His sailboat had tight living quarters.

Gadi pointed at his photographs. Jim remarked, "These are all of water and an occasional bird."

Gadi laughed, "It was boring at times, but challenging handling the weather changes. When I was on watch, I strapped myself to a safety harness in case I fell asleep."

June 24th

We saw two bright red Portuguese starfish by our yacht. Our family visited with Gadi and ate a meal together. Gadi offered, "When you get to Israel, look me up. I should be there by winter. I have family there."

Jim and Gadi shook hands. "Thanks, we'll look you up. We're sailing to Ireland, England, Scotland, and France first. Then we'll be in the Mediterranean next."

June 25th

Our fresh water tank was filled. We left Azores at 1:45 P.M. using our diesel engine due to no wind. The ocean looked like glass. I had finished checking the horizon when Alicia spotted her first ship!.

June 26th Saturday

We are now 123 miles from the Azores. The porpoises put on a great show by diving and jumping alongside our yacht. Alan started his first watch from 8 P.M. to 9 P.M. Jim approved, "Alan, you did a great job. Your Mom and I are proud of you. Would you like to take a short watch twice a day?"

Alan answered, "Sure, Dad. Can I start tomorrow?" Jim shook his head in the affirmative.

June 27th Sunday

Alan began a morning and an evening watch for one hour. This really helped us. He also gave today's Sunday school lesson.

We were still motoring at 9 P.M. when Jim contacted a Spanish ship, *Paula de Lima* on VHF radio. This was the first large ship contacted. Their radio operator said, "Give much kisses to children. We carry general cargo. We're on our way to Venice."

Jim made contact via RDF with the Russian tanker, *Mira*. It was traveling from the Baltic Sea to Santiago, Cuba.

Jim suggested, "Alan, write a note. Put the note in an empty bottle and cork it tight. Then toss it overboard."

Alan's eyes opened in surprise at the special honor. His curly brown hair blew in the wind. He got a bottle, cork, paper, and pencil. He wrote: This is the last day of my life. Alan MacGregor. Alan said, "Okay, I did it." He held up the glass bottle with his note in it. He put the cork in the opening to seal it shut.

Jim said, "Throw it over the side. Maybe someone will find your note in a different country."

Alan tossed the corked bottle over the port side. He smiled, "I want my bottle to get washed ashore. It would be neat to learn where it landed."

June 28ᵗʰ Monday

Jim woke up and was startled, "Wow, look what's following us. That's a pack of about fifteen to twenty pilot whales off our stern."

I said, "That was too close for comfort. Are we their breakfast? They followed us for half an hour.

I told Jim, "Alan was seasick last night. His has a low grade temperature this morning. He's trusting God to get him over this. What a faith."

June 29ᵗʰ

10:20 A.M. Seas started building. Bearing 60 degrees. We're on a good course. Alan is able to retain soup, water and even a few cookies. Praise the Lord!

9:30 P.M. A full moon and a light wind so we hoisted the genoa sail. Jim discussed his tentative plans. "Let's cruise Europe and the Mediterranean Sea area for one and a half years. Then we'll sail to the West Indies again and to Texas where we can store our yacht. I'll work in real estate for a year. Then we can cruise for three years to the South Pacific. We may winter this year in the Middle East."

He used to say that he wanted to be a beachcomber. *What will he dream up next?*

June 30ᵗʰ

"Look, Mom." Alicia held up her first embroidery project – an orange rose with green leaves.

"That's beautiful. I'm proud of you."

July 1ˢᵗ

High seas so we ran downwind with a working jib. The visibility was poor. Jim and I traded watch every two to three hours during the night. Jim talked with the radio operator on a large ship, *Hanatore*. "We're on our way from Tampa, Florida to Rotterdam. Your bearing at 12 noon is 48-28 North, 17-47 West. We *cannot* see your running lights!"

Later, Jim contacted Steve Jaffries a navigation officer on a Bethlehem Steel vessel. Next an engineer on the British ship, *Haverton*, gave us their phone number. Chris said, "Our ship came from Norfolk and is on its way to Ghent, Belgium. Its length is seven hundred feet with its lights rising above the water line at seventy feet. Chris verified, "Vessel on my starboard bow." Jim could see them at 3.8 miles. It broke up any monotony on a long ocean crossing.

July 5ᵗʰ

It was difficult to navigate on a misty night as we beat into the wind at a bearing of 35 to 40 degrees. Jim reported, "We'll be in Ireland today."

We anchored at 10:30 P.M. off Castlehaven, Ireland. Our family motored to shore in our hard dinghy. We tried to walk on land and staggered until our sea legs adjusted.

There on the shore about 100 yards in stood old castle ruins. The steep hills boasted of tall trees. Our kids ran up a hill, waved their arms and shouted to each other. They laughed as they played and explored the ruins.

I uttered, "What a beautiful country. This is the deepest green I've ever seen. What a treat after being on a long sea voyage, but worth it all now."

Jim advised, "We'll walk into the village up ahead. See if we can get fresh milk for you and the kids, maybe an Irish beer for me."

I swayed from side-to-side. "A nice hot meal for all of us would make the day. Jim, I'm still wobbly from being at sea for so long of a time. How're your sea legs?"

Jim blurted, "I feel like a drunken sailor, you know. Well, me lass, let's get the kids."

Our family strolled into the small village with one tavern. The villagers were dressed in casual clothes. A smiling villager shook hands with us. He said, "'Tis welcome to Ireland, that ye are. Where'd ye sail from? Gonna be here long? What nice looking children."

Jim replied, "Thanks. We're from California in the United States. We sailed up from the Azores. This is our first port in Ireland."

The villager nodded his approval. Soon other villagers gathered around our family. They invited us into their one pub and served us a hot, hearty meal. They seemed eager to learn more about us.

Alan remarked, "Mom, I can barely understand what these folks are saying. They have the heaviest accent I've ever heard."

"Son, the term is a brogue. It's an Irish brogue. Really, it's Irish English. Fresh food, wonderful people . . . I like it here. This is the richest milk." I swallowed the milk slowly to savor each sip.

Alicia commented, "It's a treat to have fresh milk. I love it here. There's lots of green . . . my favorite color. My heart wants to sing, I'm so happy."

The kids and I drank our milk and wiped our lips. I said, "The ice cream has to be wonderful." We smiled at each other and held hands.

On a wet, foggy day we decided to motor to Crosshaven Marina. We docked our yacht. Jim went ashore to get information. While he was gone, a drunken man staggered aboard *Far Horizons*. He waved his arms and ordered, "Out of my way. I'm gonna find a place to sleep. What kind of boat is this?"

I shouted, "Get off our yacht! Now! This is our home. There are small children here." I turned to Alan and whispered in his ear. "Run up the family flag. Your dad must see it. We need his help to get this drunk off our yacht."

Alan pulled the yellow plaid flag out of its storage area, climbed up the starboard shroud, and tied the flag in its place. He climbed down, came back in the main cabin and mumbled in my ear, "Our flag is up."

The drunk stumbled closer. He grabbed Alan's T-shirt and threatened him, "Where were you? What did you say to your mother?"

Alan blurted, "I told her Dad is on his way and not to worry. Mister, you're on the wrong boat. This is our home. Please go ashore. My father will shoot you if you don't."

Our family flag waved in the wind. Alan reported, "Dad saw the flag! Here he comes."

Jim rushed from the clubhouse and hurried down the dock. He boarded our yacht, grabbed the drunk by the neck and escorted him to shore. He questioned, "What are you doing here? Don't you ever come back to this yacht! I'm reporting you to the local authorities. Do you understand?"

The drunken man stared at Jim, and then pushed away from him. He slurred, "Yesh, yesh. I mish . . . taken. I leave."

Alicia rushed to her dad, and grabbed him around his legs. "Thank you, Daddy, for protecting us from the bad man. Mommy couldn't get him to leave. Alan put up the family flag so you could see it."

Jim comforted us. "Good job. The family flag works."

Later in the day, Jim and I met Irish sailors inside the marina clubhouse. We wore our yellow foul weather jackets. One Irish sailor, Patrick O'Malley, rushed to shake Jim's hand. "Pose for me, will ya? I need a picture of a real mariner. Tell us about your voyage. Have an Irish beer on me."

Jim accepted the beer. "Thanks, mate. Eleven day sail up from the Azores. Twenty-one day sail across the Atlantic from Bermuda." He laughed.

Alan and Alicia found new kids to trade books with and play games. This was an important task at each harbor.

Two days later, we sailed further north up the Irish Coast to the city of Cork. We docked our yacht at the Royal Cork Yacht Club. Alan secured the lines to the dock. Jim announced, "We're going to visit Blarney Castle tomorrow. It's near Cork. I want to kiss the Blarney Stone."

Alicia piped up, "Not me. I'm not kissing any stone. I don't want an accent."

Our family walked about the castle grounds. The Blarney Stone was embedded into the castle's highest rim. We looked up and saw a person's head upside-down who kissed the stone. Jim said, "I've been told that a person lies down on their back. You're one hundred eighty-two feet above the ground. You grab two rusty iron bars with each hand. Drop your head backward and kiss the underside of the Blarney Stone."

Alan asked, "That's high up. What does blarney mean?"

I volunteered, "I've read that blarney means varnished truth. I also read that anyone who dares to kiss it gets a gift of fair words and soft speech. Sounds like a bit of blarney to me."

Jim pointed to a Blarney Castle brochure in his hand. "It says here that the Blarney Stone is a block of limestone about four feet in length and one foot nine inches high."

Alan admitted, "I'm going to kiss it."

I told him, "Alan, you don't need to. You talk more than most people now." I laughed. Alan frowned.

Jim asked, "How about you, Elsie, are you going to kiss it?"

I replied, "No, I don't want to." I watched first Jim, then Alan kiss the stone. I resisted, but was pushed toward the stone. "All right, if I have to." I laid down on my back, and leaned backward. I held the iron bars on each side of me. I saw the ground very far below. It was scary. I got dizzy so I quickly kissed the stone. An Irishman helped me up.

He said, "Good girl. Welcome to Ireland. You'll do fine."

Chapter 8

British Isles

July 12, 1977

2 P.M. Jim filled our tank with thirty Imperial gallons of diesel fuel which is 36 regular gallons. We motored out of Cork Harbor and headed for England.

July 13th
    10:20 A.M. The sky was overcast. We traveled 104 miles.

July 14th
    We sailed up the English Channel and arrived in Plymouth, England at 6:00 P.M. where we cleared customs. Our family delighted in the plans to explore the British Isles. Our unanimous choice of our first meal in England was fish and chips. Pilgrims left here in 1620 for the new world.

July 15th
    Far Horizons left in the morning for Dartmouth. Alicia bubbled, "See the tiny castles on both sides of the harbor. I am a princess." Hills with dark green trees surrounded the

beautiful old buildings. At 5 P.M. we bought fresh milk for the children in a yacht club.

Dinner at the "Carved Angel" was served on a silver platter with English lamb and a variety of vegetables. We left Dartmouth at 10:30 P.M. and motored for Portsmouth, England.

July 16th

9:00 P.M. It was a stormy night when we docked our yacht. The next day we moored *Far Horizons* out from Hardway Sailing Club. Our passenger, Hugh, left. He had hitched a ride with us from Antigua, West Indies across the North Atlantic Ocean. The English rain persisted. Our family climbed into the hard dinghy, and Jim rowed us to shore. This was quite a shock as we shopped for groceries. I said, "I can't believe that after the clerk checked our groceries and we paid for them, she stared at us as she left the food on the counter. The market didn't have any type of bags? It's a good thing our family helped carry our groceries."

We returned to a wet dinghy. Jim rowed us back to our yacht. The groceries were soaked with rain water. We climbed aboard. I soon learned to always carry a heavy plastic or a cloth shopping bag.

We were able to take a hot shower at the sailing club. Alan asked, "Blimey, that's what I heard one of the men say. And "bloody" is another word I heard. It's a different accent from the Irish. This tongue sounds like it is twisted."

Alicia frowned as she stamped her foot. "I don't want that accent either."

I commented, "Wonderful people, but terrible weather."

Jim encouraged, "The kids will have children to play with here. We'll take some small trips to show them parts of England."

July 18th

We took a bus to Gosport to get our sails repaired at a sail maker. Finally, we had a cool, but sunny day.

July 19th

I announced, "Today is haircut day." This was a big occasion. Jim finally allowed me to cut his long hair. It was the first time his hair was cut since November of 1976. He still wore his long, ragged beard. I trimmed the children's hair as needed. There was a small laundry facility where I washed our clothes. What a relief from washing our clothes in buckets. There was a dairy near, a butcher shop and a small grocery store. I suggested, "Jim, let's get a beef roast and potatoes for dinner. This will be a feast." He nodded his head.

Jim pondered, "We could use a little car to get around England for sight-seeing. I saw 1964 Singer Gazalle car, "a bit of a banger" for sale."

I agreed, "What could we lose if we try it out? Whoever heard of a Singer car? I've only known Singer sewing machines."

He replied, "We only need it for three weeks. Let's give it a trial run."

The "Bit of a Banger" was in sad shape with its license plate attached to the fender by one bolt. Its accelerator was only a narrow strip of metal. The upholstering was torn and dirty plus the carpet was full of holes.

July 21st

Jim bought the Singer car for sixty pounds. He drove it to Portsmouth. It coughed badly when it finally started up. I retorted, "Jim, this car is so dilapidated. The clutch just went out! Will this last us until the end of the week, let alone for three weeks? Guess what, Jim. You're the only driver for this car!"

Alan exclaimed, "Look, Mom! There's a man pulling a milk wagon behind him as he delivers milk. Don't they have a horse or a car to pull the wagon?"

Alicia blurted, "There's someone pushing bread in a wire basket cart. This is like being in a farming area."

Jim laughed, "We'll be leaving tomorrow for London."

July 24th

Jim drove the "bit of a banger" for us to see horse guards changing, Buckingham Palace, Piccadilly Square, and Westminster. He announced, "We'll head for Scotland in two more days."

July 25th

I asked, "Jim, I need to find a bookstore." The first marina was in Hamble, England which also had a small bookstore with one shelf of Christian books. This was like an oasis in a dry land for me. I was parched for Christian fellowship.

July 26th

I went to Portsmouth by ferry and bought a beautiful, mauve two piece slack suit. This was a special blessing. I wore shorts and a tank top in warm weather. Slacks, a sweat-shirt, and a wool cap proved to be in order for cool weather.

July 28th

We tried whelks (a large marine snail). They looked awful, but tasted good. We finally found peanut butter and popcorn.

Alicia and Alan played with a bunch of kids. She said, "I was looking into a stream with mud flats. One kid wanted to be smart and he threw a brick to splash me. Well, it didn't splash me. It hit me on the back of my head. I shoved the brick off my head and I threw it into the water and ran down to the dock."

"I screamed at the top of my lungs when I saw the blood. Our yacht was far out there and I was bleeding a lot. It felt like my hand was inside my skull. My hand came out blood red, covered with blood up to the top of my fingertips. I screamed and was so scared. I don't remember anything except blacking out. Somehow I got to the yacht. Somebody must have calmed me down, but I don't know who. I know it wasn't Alan."

July 29th

Jim drove us to Scotland where his grandfather had built ships. Alan asked, "Dad, when will we find Ron and Jane from *High Seas*?" They had sailed across the Atlantic also and were now living in Palneckie, Scotland. They had loaned us some foul weather gear and we wanted to return the jackets.

July 30th

We went to a barbecue with Ron and Jane. There were ninety to one-hundred people. A Flounder Tromping Contest was being held. Ron asked, "Jim, ever caught a flounder?"

Jim replied, "No, what are they like?"

Ron instructed, "A flounder is a very flat salt water fish. They have two eyes on one side of the head to look up from their hiding place. It camouflages itself by lying in sand or mud. Their back is mottled and can change colors. They have sharp teeth to grab their food. It's a tasty fish. A flat fish can move in the mud."

Jim asked, "How do we catch one?"

Ron explained, "This is a narrow inlet where the tide rises and ebbs. They are easier to catch in a rising tide. Want to try it?"

"Let's do it, Ron."

I watched from a distance. I could see men stomping the mud. Jim moved about as he stomped his feet. Jim walked out of the mud first. "This is crazy. Elsie, let's leave."

I marveled, "Wow, the people here are the hardest to understand. They seem to roll their tongues. I want to shake my head to straighten out the sounds. I can't grasp what they're saying."

July 31st

Jane and I attended the Church of Scotland which was built in 1834. The church was cold and made of gray granite. It was a formal service. The local houses were also made from local granite. Later that afternoon, Ron and Jane, and our family went to see their yacht.

Jim groaned, "What a tragedy to see *High Seas* standing in a narrow ditch high and dry in the mud." It was sad see this wonderful vessel not being used. I wondered how it got here so far from the ocean.

August 2nd

Jim stopped the car at the Balquhidder Kirk. He said, "Help me find where my ancestors, Rob Roy MacGregor and his family were buried." We found the graves of Rob Roy and his wife, Mary, and two of their sons. We drove around Loch Lomond and into Rob Roy country.

August 6, 1977

I announced, "Today is our one year anniversary of living on our yacht. This has been the hardest year of my life."

Jim replied, "It's been the best year of my life."

August 9th

Jim wrote to Dick & Mary. Had a great time touring Scotland in our "bit of a banger" – a 1964 Singer car. Put on about 1500 miles. I have a money problem. So far haven't received a check. We can't move on until these funds arrive. Please look into it. Thanks. Jim

August 28th

I wrote to Mary and Dick. Thank you so much for taking care of the financial transfer of funds. We did receive the money on Saturday and are able to get the last minute marine and food provisions before setting off for France. We'll have our mast dropped at LeHavre.

August 29th Gosport, England

Letter to Marilyn Clay. Still here – just painted our hull white and our boot stripe blue. We're back on a mooring. We have been in England for 43 days. We leave this Friday for France. We'll enter the canals at LeHavre, go to Paris, and then on to Lyon. We'll leave our yacht there and drive to Switzerland. Then we'll return and continue on our way to Marseilles and enter the Mediterranean from here.

Those precious aerograms mean so much to me! You all minister to me by your notes. I do miss and love you all. I can scarcely wait to get to Israel. I never dreamt I'd ever get such an opportunity. Jim plans on going to Egypt first. We'll visit Israel for two months. Meeting some very exciting people. We never know who will come rowing up to our yacht, or rafting up, or swimming by. Love, Elsie

Jim remounted the wind vane and put up a new American flag at the stern. "Lord, I want to meet Corrie Ten Boom and pray with her. I'm desperate for Christian fellowship." I had started reading her book, *In My Father's House*. This was a blessing to my thirsty soul.

August 31st

The car muffler was shot, so Jim replaced it. He said, "Now with our new running light at the top of our mast, we should be visible to ships at sea." We placed the mainsail back on the mast. New floorboards were made for the cockpit.

A gift had been placed in our cockpit. It was a English stoneware jar with a lid and a tag that said: "Good sailing, Ken and Gordon." The jar was filled with homemade chutney. We had never tasted chutney before. It was a precious gift.

September 1st
Alan beamed, "Okay, family. I wanted to surprise you. I've cooked eggs for the first time. One scrambled and three sunnyside up. Come and eat." He did a good job. Later he went for a kayak ride.

September 2nd
The last two nights Alicia prayed, "Dear Lord, please heal Mom's left ankle and heel. Help the skin to start sticking on her foot so it won't bleed anymore."

Jim started to drive to London. He never made it. The "bit of a banger" broke down about twenty-five miles away. Jim told me, "The banger went bang!" He took the car back to Fareham and left it. He rode a bus back to the Hardway yacht club. Jim sold the car back to Bill (the same person he bought it from).

He announced, "I'm catching a ferry to Portsmouth to get some navigating charts."

Jim gave me a Hardway Sailing Club pin. "Thanks, Jim. That was thoughtful of you." Tom gave one to Alicia and one to Alan.

September 3rd
Our yacht is readied for sea. A farewell surprise party given to us from the dear people at Hardway. "We've grown to love you as our family." I was presented with a large bouquet of flowers with a gold trim. Jim was given a Hardway Sailing Club necktie from Ken, Gordon, Steve, Walton,

Marion and others. A pink stuffed animal was Alicia's gift. Alan and Alicia received two silver jubilee coins apiece from Ken.

We left at six o'clock this evening. It was a calm night with half a moon and the stars were out. We took turns on watch as we crossed the English Channel to France. Captain Jim proclaimed, "We'll be taking the sails down and the mast lowered in France to enter the canals."

Chapter 9

Submerged Dangers

Three weeks later, we sailed from England's southern coastline across the English Channel to Le Havre, France. We paid to have our mast and rigging lowered and secured to the coach roof and deck of our yacht, *Far Horizons*. The journey began through many French locks in the River Seine. Alan said, "This is so easy in the canals. What a change from the ocean."

I rejoiced, "The trees are so graceful. Children, look at that majestic chateau. I love France. Cooking and sleeping will be easier in the canals and rivers."

Jim remarked, "The French bread and cheese are the best. The local wine, ah." He smacked his lips.

Alan said, "I like it because we can get on and off our yacht whenever we want to now ... unless the water level is being raised or lowered."

I asked, "Is there anyone to thank?"

Alan and Alicia both yelled, "Jesus!"

I agreed. "Yes, remember the song: 'Jesus loves me'. How do you know that?"

Alicia answered, "The Bible tells me so."

September 12th

We motored into Paris, France. What a grand sight to see a miniature Statue of Liberty along the canal route. We docked near the Louvre Art Museum and close to the Eiffel tower. Notre Dame Cathedral was in sight. We toured Paris with the children.

I purchased a unique calendar of famous paintings of ships. The prints of French Naval vessels under sail looked majestic. What a find! This calendar was pinned to the bulletin board in our main cabin. When I turned to March the picture showed a disastrous ship being overturned in a storm. I immediately felt sick in my stomach every time I looked at this picture. "I need to rip this page off this calendar," I said. "Why March?" I felt a sense of foreboding. We stayed in Paris four days.

September 17th

Far Horizons started the day by going through some small locks. We tied up to a barge and took a train from St.Maurmes to Fontainebleau. Jim instructed, "All the kings of France have lived here." We strolled through the gardens and the palace. The huge chandeliers, art work, furniture, ceilings and floors were breathtaking. We walked back to the train station and returned to our yacht.

Jim has been more loving to our family the last two days.

September 18, 1977

We motored through sixteen locks today. Jim reported, "Trouble with our gear shift, I'll have to fix it before we can continue."

One lock keeper ignored us as he hugged and kissed his girl before he would open the lock. Our six foot keel hit mud a few times in the shallow locks.

A guy started opening a lock on one side. Then he dashed toward a car and sped off. We ran aground. He came back and opened the lock. He and another fellow opened the next three locks. One took off on a bicycle and the other man drove away in a red car.

At Montargis we went up fifteen feet in the highest lock. We entered Canal De Briane and could hear bells from a church.

September 20th

We encountered timed locks where some went up 21 feet, and another twenty feet. A lock keeper closed a lock for lunch so we had to wait. At the next series of locks, the water level went down which made it easier to control our yacht. We entered Canal a La Loire and stopped for the night at the town of Briare. Alan cooked pancakes for our breakfast for the first time. "Here, Mom, you get served first." A group of children greeted us with their teacher. They drew our flag and our yacht. They waved goodbye.

I peered over our starboard side and shouted, "Jim, we're high over a river! Is this a bridge canal? I didn't know there was any such thing. This is terrifying! There are trees and a river way below us! I hope this bridge doesn't collapse with all the weight of the water and our yacht on it!"

Jim checked the chart. "It's called Ponte Canal De Briere, and it's sixty-five meters long! It says this is the longest bridge canal in Europe."

Alan shivered, "This is weird. I hope we make it across safely."

September 28th

I reported, "Jim, Alan hasn't been seasick since we entered the French canals. I'm so glad to see him feeling better."

October 9th

We tied up to a canal in Lyon, France. This city had many old cathedrals. No drinking water will be available until tomorrow. There were very few barges or boats on the Soane River.

October 10th

We filled our tank with diesel fuel, and were able to get fresh water to fill our water tank. A gentleman approached our yacht. He introduced himself, "I'm Monsieur Jacque Bosle. I have a yacht, *Mikado*. It is fifty-four feet long. It's docked elsewhere." He handed Jim a 3"x 5" card with his name, address and phone number on it. The card read: My wife and I would be happy if you could go to our house for eating in this evening. I shall go to your boat on 8 P.M. Sincerely.

Jim and I both replied, "Yes, that would be nice. Thank you." We both were surprised at such a generous invitation.

Jacque left. He returned a few minutes before eight in his automobile. We arrived at a walled area and entered through a large door and into a dark courtyard. I held my breath, "This is a very old building. This seems surreal. There's an outside spiral staircase with stone steps going up each floor. This feels like a hundred years ago." There were several floors. We entered the living area and the dining area. The bedroom was up another floor. The children's bedroom was on the top floor. To get to a different part of their home, it was necessary to go outside and climb up the spiral staircase to each floor.

"I'm a jeweler. I have my business here on one of the floors." Jacque showed us his office. Our family was impressed with this unusual arrangement of a home.

Danielle served us an excellent dinner. Jacque related, "Eighteen thousand Christians were martyred at Lyon."

Danielle offered, "Tomorrow I'd like to take your family on a tour of Lyon and to the Basilica. Later in the afternoon we can take the funicular. This is a mountain railway pulled by cables. This will bring us up to the Roman Theatre." We agreed.

October 11th

After the day's tour Jacque and Danielle visited us on our yacht. Jim questioned, "We want to visit friends in Switzerland. Is it safe to leave our yacht tied up in this canal for about five days?"

Jacque volunteered, "I will watch your yacht every day until your return."

We decided to trust him and we gave him Norbert and Lilli's address and phone number in Lucerne, Switzerland. We had become friends when Jim and Norbert were working in New York City many years ago. They are citizens of Switzerland.

October 13th

We rented a white Renault 5 and drove to Switzerland. It had been several years since we had visited with Norbert and Lilli Ganz. Jim noticed, "What spectacular snow-covered mountains. Look at the Swiss cows with those large bells around their necks."

I replied, "I really like the architecture of their homes with the curved roofs. The house and barns seem connected." Lilli and Norbert's home was modern. We took our shoes off as we entered and put on slippers. The kitchen was upstairs.

October 14th

We rode the cable car up the Rigi Mountain through the fog. Once we were above the fog, the sun came out. The Swiss Alps are spectacular. Later, we walked through old Lucerne. The outside of buildings were painted with colorful designs and figures. Jim said, "We need to get our cholera shots here before we go to the Middle East." Dr. Schmidt took care of that need.

October 15th

Jim drove through the mountain passes in the Alps. He stopped the car. "Okay, kids, go on and play in the snow for a while." They had played in the snow on our visits to Lake Tahoe when we lived in California. It was great to be off our yacht for a few days.

October 16th

We arrived back in Lyon and returned the rented Renault. *Far Horizons* was safe. Jim commented, "Jacque has proved to be a reliable friend."

October 20, 1977

We steered *Far Horizons* down the Seine, and the Saone Rivers. Then we entered the Rhone River with a forty mile stretch not tamed by locks. This wild river contained rapids and were only six feet deep in spots. Motoring speed: ten to fifteen miles an hour. Suddenly, the water depth dropped to eighteen inches. *Far Horizons* slammed against a submerged rock wall. Jim yelled, "Hang on!" Our yacht (thirteen tons) plowed through ten more feet of rocks with its six foot keel. Scraping and crunching sounds shattered the atmosphere.

Jim was thrown over the helm. His body hit the hatch and threw him down into the main cabin where his back scraped against the fathometer. I shouted, "Jim, are you okay?" Blood spattered from cuts on the center of his forehead and right cheek. He climbed back into the cockpit.

He wiped the blood off his face and answered, "I hit my head and bruised my knee, butt and back."

I had been fixing sandwiches below when I was thrown off balance and my head struck the galley shelf. I moaned.

The yacht listed to starboard and shuddered. I yelled, "Oh, my head hurts! Are you kids okay?" The left side of my forehead and cheekbone were bruised.

Alicia sat at the dining table as she held onto the edge. Her eyes were wide open. She stammered, "Mom, Dad. I'm scared! What's happening?"

Alan was in the main cabin and he got hurled against a plastic pail which broke. He checked Alicia and said, "We're okay, Mom."

I sponged the blood off Jim's face, neck and arms. Jim tried to keep his balance. "I can't believe we're not holed. We're stuck. Let's get an anchor out, and then try to winch it in to pull us out." Jim and Alan rowed out in the hard fiberglass dinghy and dropped a Danforth anchor off the stern. They tried for three hours to get *Far Horizons* off the rocks, but the current held us fast. They attached a two-inch thick line to the winch. The line snapped and broke. The Danforth anchor sank. The river current continued to hold our yacht against the rocks.

Captain Jim decided, "Need somebody to pull us off the rocks. Flag down one of the barges. They might be able to pull us off." We waved our arms toward the barges motoring upstream. "Ahoy, we need your help!" Our yacht started listing to starboard.

Alan in frustration said, "Can't they tell that we need help?"

Alicia frowned and reported, "Mom, you've got a black eye."

I reassured her, "It's sore, but it will heal. I'm so glad that you and Alan weren't hurt."

Alan spotted a vessel in the distance. "Here comes a barge. The bargeman is holding up a thick rope. Maybe he's going to rescue us." Alan waved his hands as he leaned over the safety rail.

The barge, *Ossa*, drew closer to *Far Horizons*. The bargeman, with a heavy tan and a deep voice called out. "Catch this towline. We're going up river. Can't pull you out in the way you were going to get you off the rocks. You should have hired a pilot to guide you."

Two Frenchmen, in old clothes, motored over in a small boat. They held out a thick towline. They hollered, "Here. Our bateau has been scraping bottom for three hours as the water is too low. Catch this towline; attach it to your bowsprit. We'll try to pull you free of the rocks."

Jim caught the three-inch heavy towline, and fastened it securely to the bowsprit. Then he yelled back, "Okay, pull us out!"

Our yacht tilted, jerked, groaned, and screeched as the keel scraped across ten feet of rocks. The bargeman increased the power in his engine. Our yacht listed to port and shuddered with an awful sound before it was released. Jim tested the helm, "Steering seems okay. Let's try the motor." He turned the engine over. "It's working. We'll recover." We all breathed a sigh of relief.

Far Horizons was forced to follow behind the old barge. After a couple of miles, the barge pulled over to the side of the riverbank. The bargeman said, "You'll have to stay tied up to us until the river rises. We can't go any further upstream, and you can't go downstream. We're stuck here together. You owe me money for pulling your yacht out. I want ten thousand francs."

Jim's jaw dropped as he shook his head. He went back to our yacht and climbed down into the main cabin. We held hands and stared at each other. I took a deep breath, "Tell me the news. I'm glad we're off the rocks and floating."

"He won't release our yacht until we pay him. He told me ten thousand francs. That's two thousand dollars. We don't have it for a half hour's work? I even offered you to him. He's crazy."

"No, you weren't serious about giving me up! What else could we give him? We need the money we have for our needs. Prayer is the only answer. We need God to intervene in this situation." I closed my eyes. I asked, "Lord Jesus, take over this situation and help us through this dilemma. I honor you and praise you. Thank you. This is difficult to bear, but I want you to be glorified." Jim watched me and nodded his head in agreement.

I suggested, "I know. Let's offer him food and clothes for his family. We can only afford to give him forty American dollars."

Jim wondered, "I don't know if he'll take it. We need to be friends with the family. Let's go and talk with them." We approached the bargeman.

Jim asked, "May we come aboard to talk with you?"

The bargeman rubbed his chin and growled. He hesitated, then nodded and decided, "Come aboard."

We stepped aboard the bateau and hoped for a peaceful solution. He held out his hand, "My name is Michael Daniel Ossa."

"The same name as your barge?" I marveled at his answer.

"Yes, but of course. Come inside. We call it bateau instead of barge. Meet my wife, Shirley. These are our two children, Pierre and Francine."

The inside of the bateau boasted beautiful mahogany panels and doors. A built-in cabinet displayed quality dinnerware. Jim and Michael started a discussion about the price. Jim said, "You can't charge me a ridiculous price."

Michael retorted (in French), "You rich Americans. You can afford it! I'll squeeze it out of you."

Jim fired back, "I don't have that kind of money! There wasn't any contract!" His real estate expertise came into use.

Michael shot back, "You tightwad! Where would you be now if I hadn't rescued you?" His face turned red as he muttered to himself.

Michael yelled at Jim in French. Pierre tried to interpret. Michael relented, "All right. I'll drop the price to one thousand francs. Next time I'll leave you on the rocks."

Jim explained, "We live on our yacht. This is not a tourist trip for us. Our yacht is our home like your bateau is your home."

Michael retorted, "My family is a three generation bateau family. Other relatives live on six different bateaus. We have a school bateau for the children. There's a hospital bateau."

More discussion and bartering about the price took place. Jim pleaded, "It's impossible to raise one thousand francs for us. Please understand." Jim and I returned to our yacht.

October 21st

It was an uneasy night with much noise from the canal workers. I prayed, "Lord, I don't know what our outcome will be, but I desire to praise and thank you. My emotions are difficult to bear. I choose to trust you, Lord. I want you to be glorified."

Our family walked to tour the town and met an Egyptian man who spoke perfect English – an angel in disguise? He wore a suit and on his head he sported a plaid cap. We walked across a bridge. The water level had dropped and we could see the rocks where we had hit them.

Alan noticed, "Our yacht looks like a toy compared to the size of the barge."

We sorted through our belongings and decided what gifts to give Michael, Shirley, and their children. That evening we approached them. Jim offered, "We brought gifts for your family." Jim gripped two large bags of groceries. I carried a beautiful shawl and a box of jewelry. Alan held clothing, and some kitchen tools. Alicia brought sheets for their beds.

Jim held out the groceries, "Will this be satisfactory to you? I also have forty American dollars that I can give you."

Shirley resisted, "I won't accept your food." Her husband took the forty dollars.

I appealed, "I am delighted to share this food with you. Please receive it as a peace gesture. I want to be your friend."

Barriers were broken. Michael and Shirley accepted the gifts. "I will accept. You are released. Now be friends. I'll let you know when it's safe to depart. We go north, you go south." Michael asked us to sit down, and Shirley served us coffee. She showed us their family photographs.

Michael related, "This bateau was built in 1932. It was sunk in World War II by an American bomb in nineteen forty-four. Nine months later, it was raised and restored."

Shirley wore a smile and held out a gift. "Elsie, I'm giving you this French doll with a matching green crocheted dress, hat and parasol as a remembrance of our family."

"Merci, I will always remember you. Thank you again. Goodbye." I replied as tears formed in my eyes.

We shook hands and returned to our yacht. Jim was exhausted. He went to bed early.

We waited five days for the river water to rise higher. Jim sighed, "Only twelve more miles to go and then we'll be in deeper water of about eighteen feet or so. It'll be comfortable to get to the Mediterranean and out to sea in deep water where it's safe."

October 22nd

We shopped in a village for stamps and finally found baking powder. Alan's allowance was raised to one dollar a week. Jim and I wrote letters.

October 25th

The river level rose. We hired a "friendly" pilot recommended by Michael, to guide us down the worst part of the

Rhone River. The yacht, *Far Horizons*, and the bateau, *Ossa*, motored in different directions. After more than two hours, the pilot left our yacht at the end of the dangerous section of river and waved goodbye.

I poured out a simple prayer, "Thank you, Father, for delivering us in our time of need. Thank you that you turned around the situation and now have given us friends."

We entered a lock at 3:45 P.M. with a fifty foot drop, then another lock with a second fifty foot drop. When the water flooded the lock, we tried to protect *Far Horizons* hull from damage.

We arrived at 6 P.M. near Valence, France and Jim tied our yacht up to a bateau that appeared to be deserted. Our family retired for the night. A loud noise woke us. We heard music, and shouts. Colored lights blazed from the rim of the bateau's overhang. All of us rubbed our eyes. I said, "The bateau is all lit up. The people are dancing."

Jim answered, "It's a discotheque."

Alan asked, "What's that?"

Jim replied, "A place where people dance to recorded music."

I ordered, "Back to bed. We leave in the morning."

October 26th

We started our day at 7:40 A.M. and at 9:15 A.M. *Far Horizons*, entered a forty foot lock. At 10:40 A.M. we lowered into a forty-five foot lock, and then the water gushed out from one lock into a different lock. I declared, "This is beautiful mountainous country." From Noon to 1:15 P.M. we waited for one more lock to open. Dark clouds released their rain.

At 1:30 P.M. A sixty-five foot deep lock opened up. This was getting scary as other larger vessels were sharing this lock. Jim and I lost our balance from the strong flow of water that flowed from one lock into this much deeper lock.

At 3:30 P.M. An enormous lock of ninety feet deep with a tremendous surge of water forced our yacht suddenly against the canal wall. Our overboard rescue pole fell into the river between our yacht and the canal wall. Jim grabbed Alan. He instructed him, "I'm going to hold you upside-down by your ankles between the yacht and the wall of the canal. Grab the overboard pole as fast as you can. I'll pull you up before the water shifts again."

I was panic-stricken and implored Jim. "No, Jim! Please, don't do it. Forget the pole. Our son's life is in danger. He could be crushed to death!"

Jim ignored my plea, and he pushed Alan toward the edge of our yacht. He grabbed his ankles and flipped him upside-down. Jim lowered Alan into the canal. The yacht swayed out from the wall briefly. Alan grabbed the pole, and shouted, "Dad, I got it!" Jim pulled Alan up in seconds before the yacht swung back against the canal wall.

Alicia asked, "Are you okay, Alan? I was scared for you."

"I'm okay, Sis." Alan smiled.

We continued to motor our yacht through the rest of the canal locks toward Port Saint Louis, France.

October 27th

Into Avignon and we tied up to a charter boat, *Princess*. We were invited over for coffee by Hans and Anneliese. Their Dutch cook served us a delicious cake with pineapple and whipped cream. What a treat for our family. Hans waved his hands to demonstrate his humorous conversation. Ana spoke only German. *Princess* chartered for eight people for a stay of ten days. A crew of six completed the service and operation of this great charter river boat.

We were warned of a swell coming in two to three hours. The crew on *Princess* dropped anchor at ten A.M. Hans and Ana visited us for tea on *Far Horizons*. Our fresh water tanks were filled.

October 28th

It was a sunny day, so our family walked through the city of Avignon. Narrow streets and a rock wall circled the old buildings. We visited the Palace of the Popes, where gigantic old tapestries hung on the inside walls of different rooms. In the Grand Chapel of the Popes, I sang the chorus "What If It Were Today?" to hear the excellent sound in the chapel. I marveled, "What a privilege to see the work of so many artistic people."

In the afternoon we rode a minibus to Arles and saw an arena where Christians were fed to lions. Jim asked, "Alicia, Christians were fed to lions down there. You don't want to be a Christian, do you?"

I shuddered. *Why would he scare our five-year-old daughter?*

October 30th

Musee Cahvet built between 1745 – 1755 was our last stop. We motored from Avignon at 10:45 A.M. We passed through the last lock of only thirty feet deep at 1:30 P.M. "Hooray, we made it!" the children shouted. At 5:18 P.M. we tied up to a dock in Port Saint Louis, France.

October 31st

The port crew mounted and raised our mast and rigging. We had traveled the entire length of France through their canal system. Alan yelled, "There's the American yacht, *Audacious*! Let's go over to talk with them."

We helped Ann and Bill Carl with their mast and visited them again in the evening. They were from New York. Bill had designed hydrofoil ships and windmills for power at Grumman Aerospace Corporation. Jim and Bill discussed charts and their next destinations. Ann was the first U.S. woman to fly a jet airplane. She worked as an Air Force test pilot in World War II. "I bubbled, "Ann, your yacht is so modern. It's sleek and well-designed. It looks totally equipped."

Our family hiked into town for supplies and groceries. Alan walked away and turned a corner while we were at an outdoor market. He fled back to the market with a shocked look on his face. "Mom, Dad, did you hear those shots? I saw two men in a brown car lean out the car window. One of them had a rifle. He fired shots out the window at a black car that drove down the street."

Jim ordered, "You'd better stay close to us." All of us raced around the corner to the other street. There wasn't any sign of the brown or the black car in the street. Broken glass was all that was seen in the road.

Chapter 10

Mediterranean Medley

November 4th

J im and I reefed the mainsail and hoisted the jib as strong winds and waves were building. Our wind vane broke at midnight. We took turns at the helm. The next day we sighted Sardinia with its peach-colored rock cliff with red streaks on it.

November 6th

Our family walked the narrow cobblestone streets in Alghero, Sardinia. The fish market, the fruit and vegetable market, plus other shops were small. Alan pointed, "Look, Mom, people are hanging their clothes across the streets from one old building to the other."

November 8th

We left Alghero at noon on a sunny day. We hoisted our genoa, Charlie. I had traded for a book, *Beyond Ourselves*, by Catherine Marshall. I sensed an attitude problem and I asked, "Dear Lord, please help me to change my critical voice. This cruising life has been difficult. I desire to express your love. I so need Christian fellowship. Cleanse me for your glory."

Jim decided, "We'll continue past Sardinia and head for Malta." We passed many ships during the night.

It was a five day sail to Malta which used to be called Melita. We arrived here at four o'clock in the morning. The Apostle Paul was shipwrecked here in A.D. 60 (see Acts. 27-28). I said, "Oh, it's so great to find people to speak English with again and to see foods with English labels on them."

We went out to dinner with friends, Brian and Peggy Greer from their yacht, *Lady Vagrant*. Jim had stewed rabbit. He said, "I heard that rabbits are raised here for food. This is good food."

In the morning, Alan went ashore and caught a twenty inch long fish. He grinned, "I like Malta." With his allowance he bought a Lone Ranger man and a model airplane.

November 17th

We took a bus to Valleta. There was a stone wall that surrounded this old city. The buildings were made of limestone. There were numerous religious statues on the buildings.

On Sunday I invited Jim to Sunday school. He replied, "I don't want my mind put in a straitjacket."

Later I read, "The Lord will perfect that which concerneth me ..." Psalm 138:8

Alicia blurted, "These people's noses look like penguin's beaks." She had wanted to learn cursive writing. She wrote her own name in cursive writing today. A little victory won for our smallest crew member.

November 25th

Alan chuckled, "I have two new friends. One is David and the other is Richard. I'm going to trade books with

Richard. We're going to the Armory to see old weapons like crossbows, guns, cannonballs and armor."

November 29th

Alicia made up her own beautiful songs about the Lord! What a blessing.

December 2nd

Jim was ill with intestinal problems. He slept all day.

Joy sank off the coast of Sicily on the 29th of November. A life raft half-inflated was found. All were rescued.

December 5th

We rode a bus to Mdina, Rabat. There we met with a Franciscan Friar who showed us the beautiful St. Paul's Mdina cathedral and St Paul's catacombs from 1096.

December 9th

We left our berth in Malta and motored out of the harbor. Rain with lightning flashed during the night. By 7 A.M. we turned our engine off and raised the jib. Jim contacted a radioman on the ship, *City of Edinburgh*, who gave us our position.

December 11th

We were lashed by howling gales all day, so it was necessary to reef our mainsail. "Alan is still seasick, he vomited into a pail," I reported. High seas and increasing wind continued.

Jim ordered, "Elsie, take over the helm while I look for the wind gauge. Better wear a heavy jacket and warm cap." He couldn't find the wind gauge.

I confided. "Jim, I'm dizzy and nauseated. Could it be food poisoning? I'm drained … no energy." I belched and held my stomach. "Jim, you had better take over the helm. I'm sick."

Alicia whined, "I don't feel good. My tummy hurts."

I rebelled, "That does it. I am not going to sail to the Pacific Ocean with you, Jim."

Alan echoed, "I'm not either, Dad."

Jim jumped into the main cabin and came out with our camera. "I'm taking a picture of your mother." I stood at the helm with an ashen face – a historical moment when I disagreed with him. My body swayed back and forth. Jim snapped the photo. "Now you can go back into the cabin and rest. I'll take charge of the helm."

December 14th

Wind-swept seas pushed against our hull forcing our yacht back into the Mediterranean Sea. We overheard on the radio from a Danish operator, "An English naval vessel gets pushed back sixty miles. A strong weather warning of cyclonic force has been issued. Hail expected."

Helpless against the storm, we lay a hull for three days and nights. The center of the main cabin was the safest place to ride out the storms. A storm jib was impossible to put up.

I asked, "Jim, are there any ships nearby?"

He answered, "The visibility is poor. I heard on our radio that a container ship lost twenty-nine containers. This treacherous storm is called a Bora which comes down from the Adriatic Sea."

Alan and Alicia were frightened. Jim ordered, "Kids, keep your life jackets on and stay in the main cabin. You are not allowed in the cockpit."

Captain Jim was depressed due to much beating into the wind and waves. He griped, "I'll probably sell the yacht in Florida." I don't believe him.

He wrote a letter to Dick and Mary Wilson. After Malta we were told by the RAF that we had good weather and we left for Crete (belongs to Greece). Had a terrible storm and what should have taken us three days ended up taking us a week. Even the big ships had trouble. I think, however, that may have been a turning point as my crew – wife and nine-year-old son – are ready to mutiny and jump ship if we continue on to the South Pacific. So I'm afraid the handwriting is on the wall – cruise the Med, back to the Caribbean, then Florida (maybe California). Sell the boat and back to opening escrow. But it still means another year and a half of freedom – escape – adventure. Jim

December 15th

We continued to motor as the wind blew directly at us straight out of the east. Alan shouted, "Land Ho!" when Crete was sighted at 7 A.M. At 11:30 P.M. our diesel fuel tank was empty! Our reefed mainsail and a jib were hoisted.

December 16th

We were outside of Souda Bay at 5 A.M. when Jim decided, "We'll wait until dawn." First, there wasn't any wind, and then suddenly circles of wind gusts swirled around our yacht. This was maddening. We could see mountains partially covered with snow. At 12:15 P.M. Jim put our dinghy overboard and mounted the two horsepower Seagull engine on it. We climbed into the dinghy and rode within view of the dock when the small engine quit working. Jim reported, "It took us seven days to get here."

A sailor informed us. "There is a ferry that runs from here to the mainland, but it hasn't run for five days due to bad weather." At this point our family was exhausted.

Jim questioned, "We need diesel fuel and fresh food for my family. Where can I get supplies?"

We cleared customs. I noticed, "What lovely people. They are very efficient here. This is a nice change from the

customs personnel we've met in otl
breakfast at two o'clock in the aftern

December 17th
    We caught a bus to Hania where
fresh oranges, apples, tangerines and
marveled, "The oranges are as large ɛ
the best oranges and apples I've ever eaten. The old buildings were painted with bright colors like one sees in Mexico.
Beautiful orange trees lined the road side. Jim carried twenty
gallons of diesel back to our yacht.
    Alan and Alicia got a short ride on a tugboat to their
delight.
    Our family went out to dinner at Timokatanoroz-Emitati.
We were served liver chunks with lime, grape leaves stuffed
with rice, fresh fish, salad and cheese. Two Greeks played
bouzoukis, and one played a violin.

December 18th
    Jim bled our diesel engine several times and it still didn't
work. He said, "I'll replace the lift pump and the battery
tomorrow."

December 20th
    We shopped for groceries in Hania in a heavy rain. Our
dinghy was flooded when we got back to the dock. Choppy
waters thrashed our yacht in the harbor. There was still no
success with our diesel engine.

December 21st
    The children and I made Christmas cookies. Today was
important as we were bombarded with eight to nine guests.
Several people brought gifts for the children. Alicia was
given a skein of yarn. A fellow cruiser brought books, nuts
and candy for Alan and Alicia.

er 25th

lan beamed, "Mom, I have gifts for the crew on *earwater* including a Christmas tract." He gave gifts to Tom and Gilly Kolz, Valerie and John Rahtz, Robin Murray, and Linda Symons on *Shearwater*.

I said, "God, you are so good. I am so selfish."

Christmas day was sunny with a clear sky. Jim gave me a white wool sweater and matching cap, plus a pair of slippers.

December 26th

Jim heard his name called the last two nights. He wondered, "Who could have been calling me?"

Alan finished his model airplane, a Sabre Jet.

December 29th

On an educational trip our family went to an archaeological museum and then out to Knossos – a Minoan palace built during the Middle Minoan Period from 1800-1550 B.C. Jim insisted, "During the late Minoan Period, Crete was a world power co-equal with Egypt and the Hittite empire. Let's all sit in the royal thrones and get our pictures taken. Then let's play hide and seek in the ruins."

Our water tank on the yacht was filled in preparation for our voyage to Egypt.

December 30th

We left Iraklion (a seaport and the largest city in Crete) at 12:15 A.M. and averaged six knots per hour. We motored part way and docked at Sitia, Crete at 10:45 A.M. It was difficult docking due to a strong south wind. When we got ashore a woman said, "Here is a New Year's gift of a pink geranium and a berry branch for you." This was a lovely welcome.

New Year's Day 1978

We left Crete at 10:30 A.M. with rough seas out of the harbor. We sailed downwind around the point of Crete with only a jib up. I affirmed, "I've had enough of sailing."

An aft line snapped and two other lines snapped after two cleats were broken. Jim checked our yacht for storm damage. Out to anchor at 5:00 A.M. due to a heavy surge. Hail the size of large peas pelted us in our faces and three fourths of an inch of hail fell into the cockpit. His face was glum. *Far Horizons* turned into a strong head wind and high seas. We made one-hundred-ten miles today.

A convoy of twenty-five ships was assembled in a waiting area in order to enter the Suez Canal. A group of Russian ships, and two Red Chinese ships were also in line. Alan marveled, "Dad, those ships are gigantic."

Jim related, "We have to cut in between them and the shore lights." This was a frightening night. Our home seemed so tiny near the enormous commercial vessels.

In the channel we motored past more than twelve ships on our starboard side coming from the Suez Canal. The next morning there was some light rain and wind. Our family woke up to see pretty, yellow-breasted birds with brown feathers. They had flown on to our yacht and into our main cabin. I smiled, "Have you ever seen such wonderful birds? What a great welcome." This was a contrast from having hail the day before.

Alicia giggled, "I love them."

Alan ventured, "They must be Egyptian birds."

Jim volunteered, "After breakfast and customs, let's explore town."

Both kids yelled, "Hooray! Maybe we'll see a camel."

I yearned, "Fresh fruit ... eggs, vegetables."

A customs officer at Port Said boarded *Far Horizons*. He was a dark Egyptian male in a khaki uniform. He handed an official form to Jim. He began routine questioning in a dull, official tone of voice. "Name of vessel? How many aboard? Where did you sail from? How long will you be here? Have you been in Israel? Your yacht will be searched."

Chapter 11

Egyptian Interlude

January 5th 1978

J im replied, "Far Horizons is the name of our yacht. There are four of us aboard, two adults, and two children. We sailed from Crete. We will be here several weeks. No, we've not been to Israel before."

Jim filled out the form, and handed it back to the customs officer. The officer left and went back to shore. Alan snickered, "He sounds like Eeyore."

An Egyptian policeman held a machine gun as he boarded our yacht. Alan shouted, "Dad, you better do something in a hurry!"

Jim pushed his coffee mug into the policeman's hand. The policeman moved the machine gun in one hand and the coffee mug in his other hand. He said, "I'm here to search your boat. Do you have any guns on board?"

Jim answered, "One. For protection. It's unloaded."

The policeman ordered, "Where? I want to see it."

Jim brought out the shotgun. The policeman put the coffee mug down to examine the shotgun. He questioned, "Any valuables? Drugs?"

Jim responded, "No valuables. Only prescription drugs … thyroid pills for my wife."

The policeman appeared satisfied and left our yacht.

Alan retorted, "Dad, handing him your coffee mug was a smart move. Kept both his hands busy for awhile."

The next person to come aboard was the immigration doctor. He charged, "It'll be six American dollars for me to fill out this medical report."

Jim and I moved *Far Horizons* to the local yacht club and tied it to a dock. A uniformed guard sat in a wicker chair on shore in front of our yacht with a machine gun in his hands.

I asked, "Kids, hold my hands. Jim, what's happening? Dare we get off our yacht? Is he protecting us or protecting the Egyptians?"

Jim remarked, "Take one thing at a time. Secure our yacht, and hope there aren't any problems. Let's go ashore. He'd better not touch our kids."

Donkeys, tiny pull carts, and people clanged the bells on their bicycles. What a noisy place. Horns beeped and chants were heard. Hackney type carriages passed with fancy decorations. There were people wearing turbans, head scarves and long robes. We walked about town in Port Said. An Arab bazaar sounded like a madhouse.

There were three different funeral setups. "Gold chairs inside and very elaborate cloth hangings draped from the top and sides? What is this for?" I asked.

A person nearby explained, "The chairs are for the relatives and friends to pray for the dead person for one day until they get home."

Alan exclaimed, "Wow! What a change. These people aren't real, are they? Seems like a fairy tale."

Alicia noticed, "I love the fancy clothes. Makes me feel like a princess."

Alan pointed, "Oh, oh. They'd never allow that in the United States. Passengers sitting on the roof of the bus as it's moving! And people sticking out of the windows of the bus packed inside and others riding on top! Crazy country."

We walked on shabby sidewalks littered with trash. An open air market had clothing stalls on one side of a dirt road, and food stalls were on the other side of the road. The Egyptians asked for handouts.

I observed, "Nice potatoes and oranges. The bread looks good."

We came to the meat area where beef carcasses were hung. Jim held his nose and announced, "Phew! Beef loaded with flies and hanging outside in this heat?"

The Egyptians pointed to Jim's beard and tried to touch Alicia's red hair.

The next day, Alan ran down the dock and jumped aboard our yacht. Flour covered his hands and clothing. He grinned as he gasped for air, "Mom, Dad, I got a job!"

Jim asked, "You got a job? Doing what?"

Alan blurted, "Working in an Egyptian bakery! Look what I made." He held up some fresh flat bread. "It's good. I brought some round loaves to taste. It's hollow inside. You can stuff it with beans, tuna, fried egg or vegetables."

Our family stuffed the bread with tuna fish before we sampled the bread. I approved, "Why, this is good. Thanks, son, for bringing us the bread that you made."

Jim boasted, "I'm proud of you for finding a job." Alan glowed with the praise and tilted his shoulders from side-to-side.

January 8th

We were guarded twenty-four hours a day. This is called Port Fuad in Asia and Port Said in Africa. Today we put beef, beans and onion slices inside of Alan's bread for lunch.

January 9th

I became overwhelmed with feelings of insecurity and anxiety for our family. Alicia prayed, "Please help Mommy. She needs to read her Bible every day."

January 10th

Our family was invited to tea at four in the afternoon at Mohammed's apartment. He said, "I've worked over thirty-five years for customs. My wife and two children fled to Cairo when Port Said's railway station, casinos and one restaurant were bombed in 1973."

January 11th

Alan worked at the bakery again. Alan learned how to write his name in Arabic from the right to the left.

There were crowds of poor people. Trash abounded, and there were few sidewalks. The sales people were pushy.

January 14th

We caught a ferry at seven in the morning so we could rent a taxi for the trip to Cairo. The taxi, Red Comet, had a hilarious driver. When he hit the brakes, there was a firecracker zoom sound and a bird tweet. The inside of his taxi was decorated with flamingos, parrots, a hula girl, and flowers (all plastic). Jim blurted, "This guy is a reckless driver. He's passed through several checkpoints without stopping. Now he's speeding through part of the Sahara Desert."

As we got closer to Cairo, we could see large sand dunes, many soldiers, tanks and big guns. The land appeared flat and desolate.

Cairo was a large city with throngs of people, tenements, domed buildings, and mosques. Our children went for a camel ride. Then we took them to see the Sphinx and Giza pyramids. Jim suggested, "Alan, why don't you try to climb the largest pyramid?"

Alan paused, "Okay, Dad. Sounds like a fun idea."

I responded, "That can't be legal."

Jim pressured, "Go on, son. You can do it." Alan ran to the pyramid and started the climb. I couldn't believe what was happening.

Jim yelled, "Keep climbing! Keep climbing."

I retorted, "I don't think this is allowed. Jim, do you want him to get killed? Alan, get down!"

Alan had climbed about halfway up the pyramid. He was not afraid of heights. I called, "Alan, get down! Get down!"

Jim continued to encourage Alan, "Keep climbing, son."

"Jim, he could fall. He's only a child. Alan, come down!"

This took some time, but he eventually climbed back down to the ground without being hurt.

We toured the Egyptian museum in Cairo before taking the Red Comet taxi back to Port Said. We returned to our yacht at eight in the evening.

Alan helped Alicia with the Score reading program. On Sunday Alan said, "Mom, let me teach the lesson for Sunday school." Two young girls, Paula and Amanda Whitehead, joined us on our yacht for the class. Their parents, Roy and Ann were from South Africa and Great Britain and owned their yacht, *Allegra*. They had come up the Suez Canal from Cape Town, South Africa.

January 16th

Alan got up at six in the morning. He did six pages of math, fixed his own breakfast, straightened his berth, and went to work at the bakery. What a boy! He has changed and matured so much. He had been reading the book, *Moby Dick*, and he finished reading it today.

The eggs in Egypt were small and hard to crack. I remarked, "Jim, I've hit this egg many times. The light green shell is as hard as a rock. The chickens must eat stones for food. The yolks are hard to spread. I'll be glad when we get to a country that has nice eggs."

January 18th
Jim's temperature was 103 degrees. He had been sick for four days with aches and chills.

January 20th
I commented, "It's been one year since we were in the Bermuda Triangle storms. Jim, I'm glad that you're getting your strength back."

January 21st
Jim decided, "It's a beautiful sunny day. We'll leave for Israel this afternoon. We'll have to motor until we get a good wind. *Allegra* will be sailing there also so we'll meet up with them in Tel Aviv."
Alicia came down with a cold. The night sky provided moonlight for our journey.

January 22nd
8:15 A.M. Israel was sighted. Ships were lined up outside of Ashdod. 10:20 A.M. An Israeli patrol boat met us, circled around us, and led us partway to Tel Aviv.

Chapter 12

Middle East Encounters

A handsome Israeli soldier, in his twenties boarded our yacht. He asked, "Where did you come from?"

Jim answered, "Egypt and other countries. We're from the United States and have visited several countries. Here's my passport."

The soldier examined Jim's passport and gave it back to him. He explained, "I will search your yacht. Do you have any guns aboard?"

Jim confessed, "I have only one shotgun for protection. Here it is."

The soldier searched our yacht. He ordered, "Follow my patrol boat into Tel Aviv harbor." We kept up with the Israeli patrol boat as he led us into a dangerous and tricky, small harbor entrance with a rock wall starboard side and another rock wall dead ahead. We needed to zigzag to avoid these walls. Mickey, the harbor master met us and led us into the harbor. We were greeted by the police inspector and later by customs.

Anke Weidema greeted us, "Hello, Piet and I are from Holland and our yacht is the *La Frisonas*." I've brought you fresh bread and eggs."

I exclaimed, "Oh, what beautiful, clean and large eggs! Thank you for the fresh bread. What a treat."

We weren't allowed to get out of the marina due to a computer breakdown. Two telegrams were sent (one to Haifa) to check our security. The harbor master intervened, "Your security has been cleared, so you are permitted to leave the marina."

After we entered the narrow opening into the harbor, we secured our yacht to a dock. Other cruising families were tied up at different spaces. Our children bounced off to go ashore. I instructed, "Remember where we are docked. Come home for something to eat after you've played awhile."

Alan answered, "We will, Mom. We'll check out the beach first. See you." They ran down the dock to look for new friends.

I smiled as I waved to our children and began to hum the tune to "Where He Leads Me I Will Follow".

January 23rd

Shopping for food was a big event, so our family rode the bus to the local market. Jim delighted, "Look at the lettuce, celery and large strawberries. This is a treat for the eyes as well as the stomach."

Alan was surprised. "Wow, check these gigantic radishes. I've never seen any this big. They're the size of an orange."

We loaded our arms with bags of fresh produce and took the bus back to the marina. In the morning Jim caught a bus to Haifa to get our mail at Tami and Rafi Blattner's. Lillie and Norbert Ganz had asked them to hold our mail for us until we arrived in Israel.

When Jim got back from Haifa, he took the propane tank and went ashore to fill it. He wrung his hands as he walked back. A letter stuck out of his pocket. He grunted, "The tank is filled."

During the evening Jim seated our family around the cockpit. He brought the letter out of his jean pocket. He announced, "It says here that your grandmother, Cynthia, died from a stroke. She went home to the Lord on the fifth of last month." Cynthia was Jim's stepmother.

Alan and Alicia were upset. Tears rolled down their cheeks. Alicia mourned, "I loved Grandma. She was so pretty and showed so much love for me. I've missed her so much. Maybe she can see us from heaven?"

Alan related, "Dad, you must feel terrible. I don't know what to say, except that I loved her."

I suggested, "Let's pray for Grandpa Bill. Dear Lord Jesus, please comfort and protect Grandpa. Thank You. Amen." Jim and I consoled the children.

Before we had left California, Cynthia and I prayed together while sitting on the sofa. We often had Christian fellowship. She told me, "Elsie, this trip that you are going on will be like a large fishing net that will draw many people to our Lord Jesus."

January 31st

Ann, Roy, Paula and Amanda Whitehead went with us on the bus to Jerusalem. The land was rocky and mountainous. A church group led the way and handed Jim a three foot wooden cross. He carried it partway before he handed it to me as we walked the crowded path of the Via Dolorosa. Jim said, "Let's go to the Wailing Wall. I need to put a note in it for my friend in the states." Jewish people bowed at the waist repeatedly as they prayed at the Wailing Wall. The Jewish men wore black suits with a black vest, and a black bowler hat. Each had a long curl that hung down on both sides of their ears.

Jim played a game of checkers with Alan. I read a story to Alicia before I tucked her into her sleeping bag. She prayed, "Jesus, please tell Grandma that I love her. Please help Grandpa, my Mom, Dad and even Alan. Please help the Jewish people. Thank you."

February 3rd

Heavy waves washed a car over the break water wall at the harbor. A bystander yelled, "There are two people inside!" A seaman dove off the breakwater wall and opened the car door. A man and a woman swam out of the car and made it to the beach.

Later Mickey (the harbor master) and a scuba diver rode out in a small boat with an outboard motor. The motor stopped. Alan noticed, "They're trying to tie the boat up to the breakwater wall." He ran to tell others.

Alan shouted, "Help! The boat capsized. Send another boat to help these people!" The car was now totally underwater and was blocking the small entrance to Tel Aviv harbor.

February 4th

By late afternoon the car was found and pulled ashore by a larger boat with an inboard motor.

Ralph and Ruth Hollenberg from Holland had arrived on their yacht, *Alk*. Ralph related, "I asked my wife if she'd like a full-length fur coat. You can choose the best one that you see."

She answered, "Ralph, I really don't want an expensive fur coat."

He answered, "You don't? Okay, we'll buy a yacht instead."

February 8th 1978

Before we left, I prayed with our children that the Lord's Presence would be felt and our day blessed. We rode a bus to the train station and took a train from Tel Aviv to Jerusalem.

From the train station in Jerusalem, we rode an Arab bus (a modern-day donkey) on our way to Bethlehem. Our driver and several of the passengers wore the Arab headdress and robe. The bus rattled and shook. I marveled, "I hope this bus holds together. Driver, one of the windows in front of me fell off." A passenger bent over and picked up the window and placed it back into the window frame. "Will this window fall off again?" I asked. "I don't want our children to get hurt." No answer.

Our children were oblivious to any danger. They were as fascinated as I was with the locale and the passengers. I remembered, "I have always wanted to see Bethlehem and now we're almost there. The scripture from Micah 5:2: *"But thou, Bethlehem Ephratah, though thou be little among the thousands of Judah, yet out of thee shall he come forth unto me that is to be ruler in Israel; whose goings forth have been from of old, from everlasting."* Even today the call is to come to the living bread, Christ Jesus. We are to leave the old ways and thoughts to learn of Christ. He alone can satisfy the hungry soul and offer eternal life.

I had taught our children about Jesus and both of them had received Jesus as their Lord and Savior at an early age. We went to church together. Praying for others and talking with Jesus was normal for the three of us. We got off the bus and walked to the Church of the Nativity. We bent over to enter through a low door which let people in and kept horses or camels out. Alan observed, "Don't trip. There's an opening in the floor where an ancient floor has been discovered. Alicia, look at the art on the church walls."

I was unaffected by the surroundings. We walked down to the grotto. I questioned, "Why are there so many golden hanging lamps? There's a silver star with fourteen points surrounded by white marble in the floor. Why is there a small circular dome over this area?"

My husband spoke, "That star is approximately twenty-two inches in diameter. Children, why don't you touch the spot where the star is? When you go back to the United

States, you can tell the children in Sunday School that you were here and you touched the place where Jesus was born." I was surprised to hear his suggestion.

Alan and Alicia knelt down and touched the multi-pointed silver star. They got up without a word. I thought, I'm not going to kneel down. Then I decided, if the children did it, I might as well also.

I knelt in front of the large silver star. There was a circle of water in the center of the star. Many incense burners were hanging a few feet above the star. *This seems religious. I'm not used to these incense burners.*

On impulse, I thrust my hand forward. I pressed it on the silver star. In that instant, all outer feelings left. Tears ran down my cheeks. "Oh, Lord Jesus, I feel your manifested presence. I adore you. I am truly on holy ground. I praise you and worship you! You are alive! You have given me new peace and a joy that is strengthening me. Thank you for speaking to my heart. I praise your name, Lord Jesus."

I reflected on the scripture, *"I am the living bread which came down from heaven: if any man eats of this bread, he shall live forever: and the bread that I will give is my flesh, which I will give for the life of the world."* John 6:51 KJV

"I see it now, Lord Jesus, You are the living bread. Bethlehem, the city called the House of Bread was chosen for the birthplace of the Bread of God. Christ birthed within us is our sustenance, our life." My heart was overwhelmed.

Alan and I went back ten minutes later, but a cleaning man was washing the area. So I walked over and got down on my knees in the place where the wisemen had knelt near the manger. I prayed again for my husband's salvation.

Jim snapped, "What happened? What were you doing? Let's get going."

I replied, "I lit a candle for you."

He grimaced, "Oh that makes me very angry!" He turned and pounded his feet up the stone steps. Our children and I followed behind him.

February 9th

Jim tripped in King Solomon's quarries. He moaned, "I've sprained my ankle. I was smitten down while straying from the path of light. King Solomon was no friend of mine."

I reflected, "Lord, I now have your peace and a new sense of self-control. You have given me renewed love and patience for Jim and our children."

February 10th

The train left for Haifa at eight in the morning. Jim checked for a haul out at their port. There was a two month waiting list. He decided, "We'll need to sail to Lebanon in order to paint the hull."

Rafi drove us to Akko. The Israeli houses and apartments had hot water tanks on the roofs for radiant heating. Metal shutters were on windows to keep out the sun. Tamar started teaching us some Hebrew words. Alan said, "I like *ope la* the best because it means whoops."

February 11th

Rafi and Tamar arranged for all of us to take a Hebrew tour through Cana, Mount Tabor, Nazareth, and Tiberias. He said, "We'll have a breakfast stop at the Sea of Galilee." There were banana trees, date palms, grapefruit trees, grape vines on steep slopes. The water was clean and calm at this time.

Rafi explained, "We are now going to Gamala which is the most ancient synagogue discovered in Israel so far. It was built in 67 A.D." There were heart-shaped granite pillars at the ruins. Alan got his request as we went to Mount

Carmel where Elijah's cave was located. The train took us back to Tel Aviv to complete our day.

February 17th
Our family was thrilled to meet a man called Abraham who owned a photography studio in Tel Aviv. He said, "I've invited Alan and Alicia to come to my studio to watch some Disney and other children's movies twice a week while you're still here. There isn't any charge."

We also met Gadi who we first met eight months ago in the Azores. He introduced us to his parents and his sisters.

March 7th
At seven in the morning our keel struck sand coming out of the entrance into Tel Aviv Harbor. Jim backed off with our motor until we cleared the harbor and headed toward Lebanon. An Israeli patrol boat checked our progress as we hoisted our sails and headed north.

A Lebanese P.L.O. patrol boat bypassed us during the late evening going south. Jim noticed, "We're about ten miles off the Israeli/Lebanon border. There's a large Israeli vessel with about one hundred soldiers aboard coming toward us."

Jim lifted up our large American flag and waved it. He shouted, "We're American citizens. See our U.S. flag!" The Israeli group of soldiers waved back, smiled and motored off.

I decided, "They must have checked our security clearance."

We sailed into a harbor in Lebanon and saw a large building with the Jounieh Yacht Club sign. Jim secured our yacht to the dock. He explained, "I checked with other cruising captains about the most reasonable place to work on our yacht. The majority chose Lebanon. It'll be hauled out to dry dock. Then we'll scrape the barnacles off the hull and keel before we paint it."

Our Scottish mariner, Ron Pole, in his twenties, tall, thin and handsome reported, "The P.L.O. attacked Tel Aviv during the night. You must have bypassed their patrol boat. They bombed the hotel next to the Tel Aviv harbor near the beach."

I sputtered, "Oh, no, our children played on that very beach yesterday and swam in the seawater. Thank God, we left when we did."

Jim questioned, "Wonder what the Israeli's will do in reprisal to the attack in Tel Aviv?"

A Lebanese inspector took our passports. He informed, "Mr. MacGregor, your passport is going to Beirut. We'll keep it until you leave Lebanon. You may keep Mrs. MacGregor's and the children's passports." The inspector left.

Jim wondered, "I must be suspicious looking."

I replied, "With your scraggly beard and long stringy hair, I'd say so." Jim grumbled and turned away.

March 18th

I walked into Jounieh to find a market when I came upon a small square. There was only one sculpture on a pedestal in this garden area. The sculpture was of a bearded man with a turban on his head. I read the words "Sultan" and his name on a plaque. A distinguished man approached me. I asked him, "Who is this and what does Sultan mean?"

He answered, "This sculpture honors one of our rulers. I'm waiting for my family. My daughter is choosing her trousseau." He looked across the street at one of the shops. "She should be done shopping soon."

I opened my small New Testament and started to read Scriptures regarding my Lord's Second Coming. He asked, "What are you reading?" I pointed to the verses. We started a discussion. He was fascinated with my words and he invited me to his home. He offered, "You can ride back with me and my daughter. I want to compare what you read with my

Arabic Bible. You can meet my wife. I'll give you a ride back here to the market area so you can do your shopping."

Without hesitation, I decided to trust him. His lovely daughter came to the car followed by a salesperson who carried her many boxes of new clothes. She had dark, long hair and a perfect figure. Her beautiful face was glowing. Her father introduced us and we stepped into his black automobile. He drove off. *Oh, Lord, where are we going?*

Mr. Elias drove for several miles. We walked into his house. His daughter sat down on a chair as she spread the many boxes around her. She began to take out her special clothes one by one. She held them up for me. "What is your opinion of this dress?" She sought my approval. All of her choices were excellent.

Mr. Elias left to get his son. I was able to converse freely with his wife and daughter until her husband returned with their son who appeared to be about eight years of age.

His wife served us fresh fruit and coffee. Once her husband had arrived again, the women were not allowed to talk with me. I noticed a very long tapered fingernail on each of his little fingers. Did this mean that he didn't work?

My sole purpose of coming here was to share the Bible. He brought out his very large Arabic Bible which read from the right to the left. The last page was his first page. He started from the bottom of the last page and read upward. We compared Scriptures from the Old Testament and the New Testament. He seemed amazed to hear of signs of Christ's Return. After our discussion, he said, "Wait here. I'm going to get my brother. I want him to meet you." After he left, I was free to carry on a conversation with his wife and daughter again. This was a different world.

He returned and introduced me to his brother. "It's time to drive you back to the market. I'm taking my son with us." He did as he said and I got out of his car to get some food for dinner. I walked back to the marina. Jim was ill with a stomach disorder. I never said a word to Jim about the day's adventure, because he was antagonistic about any time that I would share Jesus.

March 21st 1978

I cut Alan and Alicia's hair in the cockpit. I looked at them and approved, "There, you look better. I'll make pizza out of my bread dough today."

Alicia yelled, "Hooray, Mom!"

Our yacht was hauled out to dry dock at 3:30 P.M. Jim inspected the damage. He reported, "Elsie, most of the damage is on the port side of our keel and the bow. There's also damage on the starboard side of our hull." We oiled the teak and scraped barnacles off the hull and keel. "Okay, let's hose off this whole area with water and let it dry. We'll paint the keel and lower part of the hull with the anti-foulant paint to kill algae tomorrow. We won't have the blue stripes on the hull anymore. We'll paint it all white."

Rocket fire was heard again. Jim announced, "The reprisal has started. Elsie, I heard that Beirut used to be one of the nicest cities in the Middle East. It's a wreck now. Blocks and blocks of buildings have been shot up."

March 24th

I walked on the street near the marketplace when I saw Mr. Elias drive up in his car. He saw me and spoke to me from his car window. I handed him some Christian pamphlets. He took them. He never came to the marina. He seemed to be an important man.

March 28th

Far Horizons was taken out of dry dock and put back in the harbor. Jim filled the fuel tank with diesel. Alan beamed, "Our yacht looks great. I like it even better without the blue stripe."

Jim met Ahmed, a native Lebanese cigarette dealer. He was a sinister-looking, middle-aged man with a swarthy complexion. He pushed a blue, wooden cart down the street in Jounieh. He introduced himself, "My name is Ahmed. Would you and your family like to ride with me to Beirut in the morning? I'll show you the city, and drive you back to the marina."

Jim said, "Thanks, we'll wait for you to pick us up at the marina. See you in the morning."

The next day, Ahmed arrived at the marina and drove us to Beirut. Military tanks were stationed in parking lots and a peace-keeping force was present. Hotels stood with sections of crumbled walls and windows completely broken. There was much devastation, and street after street had been bombed. Many bullet holes were in the walls of large buildings. In a Christian section we saw three garage doors in a good area with crosses on the doors.

Ahmed said, "I know where to drive so we don't go over any mined areas.

Jim observed, "Look, anti-tank traps. Machine gun nests with sandbags in front. Stay in the car."

Ahmed spoke, "There's an underground city here. It's a military stronghold, called Telzaatar." There was a Palestinian village completely destroyed and vacant.

Alan sensed, "People die here."

Alicia cringed, "I don't like it. Can we go back to our yacht?"

I whispered to Jim, "This is insanity."

Ahmed drove us back up into the rock-covered hills east of Jounieh. There were many sheep with long hair and horns that wandered in the hills. Snow was visible on distant mountains.

In the evening Ahmed showed us his living quarters in his apartment. Very expensive hand-crafted furniture, a large Oriental rug, and fine tapestries decorated his home. He smiled, "Welcome. Please have some tea. Help yourself to the food." He served us hot tea in small glasses. He offered, "Please take some pastry, apples, or peanuts." He gave Jim a bottle of Cutty Sark. Ahmed served the kids sodas and a strange green fruit.

Jim thanked him. "It was nice of you to spend your day driving us around. Thanks a lot!"

Ahmed bowed. "You're very welcome."

On the way back to the marina, Ahmed stopped at a bakery and bought more pastries. Then he drove our family back to the marina before he left. That evening our family sat at the table as the children feasted on the pastries. Jim commented, "It looks like he has a better income from something other than selling cigarettes from a push cart."

I replied, "Yes, but what a strange man. Did you notice the tapestries and expensive furniture in his home?"

Jim pondered, "Seems like he stopped at bakeries a lot. Did he have other business there?"

March 31st

Jim hired a taxi from Jounieh into Beirut to get his passport. When Jim returned, he related the day's events. "I instructed the taxi driver to take me to the customs office. I asked him to wait for me. I would need a ride back to Jounieh. He asked if I had enough cash. I opened my wallet and showed the driver many Lebanese bills." It was a hectic ride.

I pressed, "Then what happened?"

"It was hot. Flies flew in the open window in the customs office. They kept buzzing around my head. I had to wait in line. Sweat was pouring down our faces. There was a large ceiling fan that barely rotated. When it was my turn, the officer kept tapping his pencil on the desk. He squinted his eyes as he questioned me. I was getting nervous."

Jim took a deep breath, "I told him my name and that I was here to get my passport. He wanted to know if I was in intelligence, or had any drugs on board. I explained that I was a captain on my yacht. My crew consisted of my wife and two young children. My reason for coming to Lebanon was to paint my yacht."

"What did he do? " I shuddered.

"The customs officer whispered to another officer. I couldn't hear what they said about me. I was hoping that I wouldn't get arrested on false charges. Laws are so peculiar in different countries. I know I looked like a bum."

I panicked, "What would the kids and I do without you? How would we be able to help? Jim, that's horrifying!"

"Believe me; I was holding my breath as I waited for their decision. I didn't dare move. At last, my passport was released to me. I left the customs office, stepped into the taxi and ordered the driver to go back to Jounieh. I *am* upset."

His face blanched as he explained to me, "Elsie, we *have* to hurry. Gather the kids and our stuff. We're slipping out of the harbor tonight and leaving Lebanon when it's dark."

I asked, "Why? What's the matter?"

"The way the customs officer questioned me, I'm afraid we're being watched. They might take my passport away again. We've got to sail out of the country tonight."

I disagreed, "I don't like sneaking out."

We prepared the yacht for our voyage. As the diesel engine ran at a slow speed, *Far Horizons* slipped quietly out of Jounieh harbor. Jim accelerated the engine. We looked back to see if we were being followed.

Jim sighed, "Elsie, it seems safe now. I don't see any patrol boats. We'll put up the sails as there's a good wind starting."

I sulked, "I feel like a crook … sneaking out of a harbor."

Jim insisted, "There wasn't any choice." He smugly focused on the raising of our sails.

Chapter 13

Where to Now, Captain?

April 7th 1978

We enjoyed a successful voyage to the southeast coast of Larnaca, Cyprus.

Jim volunteered, "This is the third largest island in the Mediterranean. I'll get our three propane tanks filled here. We'll all go ashore and buy fresh food."

Without refrigeration we could only purchase food supplies to last a few days. When we were docked at a marina or moored out in a harbor, the daily stops included: First, a bakery for bread and dessert; second, a store with dry packaged goods; third, a produce market; fourth, a cheese or poultry shop, and last, a butcher store.

April 8th

Alan shouted, "Here come our friends, Paula and Amanda from *Allegra*!" They arrived at nine in the evening. How great to see them again! Our cruising friends that we had met from time-to-time at other ports became our stretched-out family.

April 9th

Sonia played the guitar for the Sunday school aboard our yacht with Paula, Amanda, Andrew, Alicia, and Alan. I grinned, "Tell your parents that I'm fixing a special dinner to celebrate your arrival. Come over around two o'clock. I'm cooking a leg of lamb, American rice, zucchini, tossed salad and cake."

April 11th

Due to high winds, our attempt to leave Larnaca for the past two days was aborted. Our friends on *Alk* and *Allegra* gave us a big send off. We sailed past Limassol at 8:45 P.M. and decided to continue on. At 4 A.M. we motored until we arrived at Paphos, Cyprus at 10:30 A.M. where the shore was lined with yellow daisies and red poppies. We saw large white pelicans. Jim said, "This city was originally founded by the Phoenicians. It's a gorgeous day to walk through the ancient ruins." This was a hard way of life. I fixed cucumber and tomato sandwiches for lunch.

April 12th

We left Paphos at 6 A.M. in smooth seas. During the night we heard five or more planes in military maneuvers. Jim spotted a ship with helicopters.

April 13th

Alan wasn't seasick this trip. We noticed a U.S. jet as it flew over us twice. In the distance we could see snow on the mountain tops in Turkey. At 2 P.M. Jim tied our bow up to a wharf at Finicki, Turkey and he cast an anchor out from our stern. The high mountains were covered with scrubby bushes. I commented, "Why are ninety-seven percent of the men walking in groups?"

April 14th

Jim bought an enormous lobster from a Turkish fisherman. We motored to Kekova Demiryeri on a hot day. Our bathing suits were put on for the first time in over a year. We were in an isolated anchorage where I fixed lobster, salad, potatoes and zucchini.

Our family explored a castle with Ghibelline battlements and a tiny Greek theater. Alan questioned, "Those look like large lunchboxes? What are they?"

I replied, "They are Lycian tombs above the ground scattered along the hill tops. People were buried in these tombs that resemble houses. Some of the tombs have a roof and others might have a door. I've heard that these are only found in southwest Turkey in isolated places."

April 15th

After Sunday school, we left Lycia at 11:15 A.M. in a light rain. Jim lost his cap in an ill wind off the small Greek island of Kastellorizon. Alan wasn't seasick through this trip either.

April 16th

We docked *Far Horizons* up at Rhodes at 7:30 A.M. where three old windmills and a fifteenth century tower (that was now a lighthouse) were directly in front of our yacht. Alicia cried, "Oh, look, Mom! There's a big castle behind the windmills. I'm a princess!"

Jim responded, "It's called Castle of the Knights. I've heard that it will be all lit up with lights tonight."

Groceries were expensive. Thirty-six drachmas equaled one U.S. dollar. Alan was ill that evening. Alicia found a girl who was six and one-half years old to play with.

April 18th

Jim saw a stray yacht that was adrift in a heavy wind. He got into our hard dinghy to help rescue this vessel. Two Greeks started out in their boat to help also. They gave up and waved goodbye to Jim. Two fellow cruisers, Tom and Alan (who had only arrived a week ago) saw the dilemma and came to assist in this rescue.

The big event for our family was to experience a Turkish bath. The Turkish bathhouse was four-hundred-years-old. The wooden walls were stained green. To enter the bathing area, there was a large, heavy stone attached to a rope in front of the door. When one opened the door and entered the bathing area, the stone would make a loud noise when the door shut. Alicia shivered, "This is creepy. Where are we?"

I answered, "This is a different way of bathing. Hold onto my hand. We'll stay together."

We entered a large room with a marble floor where people were sitting and bathing. Individual changing rooms were located upstairs. The steam rooms had marble basins and marble benches. Light came in through the fancy ceiling that boasted stars and circles. Jim suggested, "Let's take a side room for our family." This worked out great. To leave we exited the huge wooden door and as the door slammed shut, the stone slammed against the green door with a loud noise as it announced our departure. Alicia and I got a free Turkish bath. The lady who worked there said, "For a souvenir."

April 20th

We departed Rhodes and passed Cornucopia at 12:15 P.M. At 6:15 we anchored in a beautiful secluded harbor, the Harbor of the Apostle Paul. We were the only yacht in the harbor. I remarked, "Paul landed here in 53 A.D. Oh, there's a small, white church called St. Barnabas church." The Acropolis of Lindos on a mountain peak was on the opposite shore. All the houses were white and appeared clean. My heart was filled with joy. I sang, "Go tell it on the mountain, that Jesus Christ is Lord!"

April 27th

We departed Rhodes and docked at Symi in a small bay. Our family visited Panormittis, a first century Greek Orthodox Monastery. We saw a man on the street holding a flat of red dyed eggs. He said, "This Sunday is our Easter Sunday." I attended the evening service which was very elaborate, ritualistic and ceremonial. The priest wore a satin, black two piece robe with a silver embroidered cross in the front along with other trimmings in silver. When he turned around, there was another embroidered cross on the back of his robe. The entire service was in Greek.

I sat in a tall, narrow chair with high arm rests along a wall. Half of the seat folded back when I wanted to stand. The people stood when the priest came out of the altar room. I could see a silver cross, flowers, and a lighted candlestick inside the altar room. At times he would put on a black hat with a long black drape attached. People came in, put a coin in a box, took a candle and lit the candle. They crossed themselves many times, and kissed the silver plaque of Michael the Archangel. Two other priests walked about, waving incense burners. Later the priest appeared with a large cross with an image of Jesus (made of cardboard) and circled the church three times around the center candelabra. Clouds of incense surrounded the priest and the cross. The ceilings and walls were covered with frescos. The priest put a wreath of red carnations on Jesus' head. During World War II the abbot was shot by German soldiers.

April 28th

6:30 A.M. We had a bad start as we hit the dock as we tried to leave Symi. There was poor wind so our diesel motor temperature ran high. We arrived outside "Castle of the

Knights" at Kos, Turkey and anchored down at 10:30 P.M. The harbor was dirty, but cleaner out by the castle. We have one propane tank out. The small one lasted three weeks. The produce was of poor quality. The small store prices were less here than at Rhodes.

April 30th

We sailed into the harbor with Genoa #3 at Bodrum, Turkey and anchored. Three different minarets could be heard. Jim filled our fresh water tank. I washed clothes on deck in pails as I sang "The Old Rugged Cross". The Lord spoke to Alicia. I changed the plaque in the galley to "Trust in the Lord". Then I sang "Swing Low, Sweet Chariot". Alan said, "Mom, that's my favorite song." He wrote the words down.

May 1st

Alicia and I walked into town. Bodrum's population was 7,000 people. I purchased bread in different shapes; as well as meat, oil, eggs, and zucchini. We met Lilah who ran the bead shop by the castle. Alicia grinned, "Oh, those are so pretty. How can I learn to make jewelry?"

Lilah said, "Here, let me show you how to string beads. I'll give you enough beads to make a necklace." Alicia's eyes danced.

May 2nd

White caps were in the harbor from a terrible wind storm. Jim and Thelma's fifty-six foot yacht's anchor broke loose. I met Thelma, Anna and Claudine so I invited them over for tea. Claudine spoke, "I've brought you this bouquet of purple flowers." What an unusual special blessing. Thank you, Lord!

I answered, "Here's a wonderful book, *The Hiding Place*. It's a gift for you."

May 3rd

Jim and Thelma came over to help fix our alternator. It needed two diodes and one lead had been poorly soldered. It was fixed in a short time.

May 5th

Women gathered for market day in the village. They wore baggy, multi-colored pants and long head scarves. The produce boasted great lettuce, cucumbers and zucchini. Jim reported, "We're leaving at noon so hurry back with fresh vegetables." Alicia and I scurried back.

We left Bodrum and ran into a fierce Meltemi storm with winds of 30 to 35 miles per hour. Jim shouted, "Our working jib jolted off the deck! We have to find it!"

My chest pounded as it kept time with the rhythm of the waves. I pressed my hand against my forehead. The waves slammed against our hull. I froze, "It could have been one of our children!" I lived in constant fear that we could lose one of our children. Alan had sleepwalked when we lived on land in California. We searched for three hours, but it had sunk. It had been in a canvas bag. We couldn't recover it. My husband, Jim, was determined to have his own way in spite of the dangers at sea.

May 6th

We motored up the Turkish coast at 10 to 12 knots. The winds increased. We turned around about 11:40 A.M. and went back to Kos to get check-in papers and transit papers for Greece.

May 7th

We left for Kalimnos which had a pretty harbor and village. The streets were very narrow. The houses looked box-like with bright trim in pink, green and blue colors. I walked about the village and up the mountainside. I found the tiniest church I'd ever been in and I felt the Lord's presence. I lit two candles and prayed as tears ran down my cheeks. "Lord, I know that you never leave me nor forsake me. Thank You."

An older woman there wore a black dress and a black scarf. I noticed, "Jim, I saw many homes that had a lamb tied up like a pet. Some homes had blood in the shape of a cross over their door frame. They must be Greek Orthodox. There must be about twelve churches in this village."

I tried to make mayonnaise today. It didn't set. So, I baked a cake instead.

May 8th

We headed out of Kalimnos at 6:00 P.M. and stopped at Kanerios Island which had high cliffs with a foreboding look. The bay was very narrow with rocks and gusty winds. Jim declared, "This is a bad anchorage! Let's check out Nisos Dhenousa Island." We got there at three-thirty in the morning. It was too dark and dangerous with only one flashing light on the peak.

May 9th

We anchored in the harbor of Nisos Naxos which was a little bay of Apollona. Naxos was the largest and most mountainous of the Cyclades. We were able to sleep from 10 P.M. to 2:30 A.M.

May 11th

On our twenty-second wedding anniversary, we sailed to Kea Island. Jim and I didn't always agree, but we were still in love. We arrived in Kea about 6:00 P.M. where we purchased fresh bananas, apples, carrots, steak and Greek candy (made in Siros). Yesterday, Alicia and I wandered in a candy store where a man gave us each a large piece of soft gelatin-like candy with nuts and covered in powdered sugar. I bought a box of this candy for our anniversary gift. After lunch we had "Loukerumi" (Turkish Delight). The mountains were terraced with green rock. Alan asked, "Is this marble?"

A man's donkey carried a basket filled with vegetables. Jim said, "Let's get lettuce and beets from him. They look great." So far most of the Greek islands have been barren with stubby growth.

May 12th

We sailed to Cape Sounion. In the afternoon we walked up the hill to see the temple of Poseidon which was made of marble. Jim suggested, "Let's sail to Kalamaki Harbor which is south of Athens tomorrow. We might see the *Allegra* crew."

May 13th

Canned goods were very expensive here. At 5 P.M. a tremendous, nasty surge tossed our yacht until the middle of the night. Our bowlines broke loose.

May 14th

Sunday school ... sponge bath ... mended clothes ... terrible docking. Jim decided, "I'm taking our forward anchor chain to be cleaned. I hope to get it galvanized."

I responded, "I really wish we'd leave here."

Dave invited us along with Roy's family over to Cal and Chuck's apartment for a barbecue. We had a feast: fat hamburgers, spareribs, junk snacks, and soft drinks. He arranged rides for the twelve of us both ways. Dave spouted Christian words in a facetious way.

May 15th

Paula and Amanda were invited on board for lunch. We sang Christian songs. Paula broke out in tears as she ate lunch. She was under conviction. Both Paula and Amanda received the Lord Jesus Christ. Paula told the story of the lame man at the gate and she sang "Silver and Gold". She copied several Christian songs.

May 17th

I announced, "Alicia, today is your seventh birthday. I've made you a sailboat cake."

She stated, "I don't need this pretty anymore. I'll give it to someone." That special blanket had comforted her for years. Dee and Dave came over for her birthday party at 2 P.M. Alicia received: jump rope, jeans, shorts, a jumper, yellow turtleneck blouse, a Minnie Mouse puzzle, a toy guitar, two coloring books, a Jesus book, a doll with long black hair wearing a wedding gown, a tiny dust pan and a whisk broom. Dave brought balloons. Alicia bubbled, "This is my best birthday. Thanks!"

May 18th

Our family took the bus to Athens and saw the changing of the Greek guards. We toured the Acropolis, and the Parthenon. Alicia and Alan had balloon fights. The streets in Piraeus were loaded every several feet with Communist posters.

May 22nd

Jim and Alan went to see a movie, "High Noon" for Alan's pre-birthday gift. When they got back, Jim reported, "The anchor chain did get galvanized, but our sails are not ready." George brought ice cubes over, beer for Jim and sodas for me and the kids. It was 82 degrees and to have a cool drink was special. Without a refrigerator we didn't expect ice cubes.

May 24th

Alicia teased, "Alan, now today is your birthday. You're 10 years old. Do I get to spank you? What are you getting for your gifts?"

Jim threw his shoe in Alan's cake and ruined it. I shook my head, "Jim, why did you have to get angry on his birthday?" We invited fellow cruisers over for a party. Alan received: two model boats, one model plane, three comic books (Huckleberry Finn, Three Musketeers, Arabian Nights); an Army set with tanks, jeeps, trucks, soldiers; a sailor outfit for G.I. Joe, a whistle with a compass, candy and undershorts. Dave gave him lifesavers and gum.

May 25th

One hundred and two liters of diesel fuel was pumped into *Far Horizons* fuel tank. Our sails were done. The Charlie genoa was made into a working jib and the light genoa edges were reinforced with pieces of the Charlie canvas.

May 26th

We motored through the Corinth Canal on a sunny day. We arrived and tied up at Galaxithi, Greece. This was a nice quiet harbor with some small evergreen trees for a change. I beamed, "I like this part of Greece the best." Alicia read two songs by herself (and sang them) out of a Beginners Song Book. One was "Oh, Give Thanks", and the other was "Praise Him".

May 27th

We left Galazithi for Itea and anchored in the harbor. Next, we took a bus through high mountains to Delphi. The bus was one and a half hours late coming back due to a flat tire. Alan perked, "Watch that man on a donkey as he drives those cows and goats." It was a joy to get on land.

May 28th

The entrance to the tiniest harbor called Naupactos was fifty to sixty feet wide and on the starboard side was a sentry box. On the port side we could see a statue of a man that held a torch as he stood in a rowboat. An old fort was up the side of a mountain.

June 2nd

This next week we sailed past many more Greek islands, including the island of Corfu. On June 7th we heard two extremely loud gun shots close by. Five minutes later, we heard distant cannon fire.

June 7th

We were off the Albania coast when at 1:30 A.M. Jim sighted four ships. He said, "I heard two loud gasps for air within a few seconds when I saw a fluorescent trail in the water to our amidships. It looked like a torpedo. It was porpoises swimming, diving and jumping alongside our yacht. With the moonlight glancing off their trail, it did look like a torpedo. This was quite a sight."

Chapter 14

Adriatic Sea Adventures

June 8th

8:15 A.M. Alan and I hoisted a jib without asking the captain. We tied up in a lovely harbor at Budva, Yugoslavia at 4:30 P.M. The green mountains refreshed our senses after being at sea for long periods of time. I said, "Let's buy some fresh fruit and vegetables to stock up with for our trip up the coast." We found small peaches, large strawberries, tiny cherries, cabbage, and lettuce. Old buildings and rectangular shaped stone walks boasted a gigantic bell (as tall as one and a half persons) outside the city walls. The weather was humid and hot.

June 9th

There was very little wind so we motored up the coast to the Gulf of Kotor and tied up at Hercegovina where we stayed overnight. The next day, we motored close to the seaport of Dubrovnik. In the distance we could see high walls that surrounded a fort in mountainous country. We moored out a short distance in the harbor at Zaton. Alicia grinned,

"Oh, look at the pretty houses." The stone fences in front of the homes were four feet high and displayed many flowers.

June 12th

The children had been swimming and having fun. Our stern anchor gave way while Jim and I sat down to breakfast. The high wind banged us into the dock. Jim commanded, "Get the kids, we're leaving Zaton this morning." We sailed under high wind and waves until we arrived at Korcula in the late afternoon.

I commented, "Alan, Yugoslavia is great! I was able to buy large, sweet cherries and even a tender T-bone steak for a change."

Alicia sulked, "If you're mean to me, I won't do anything for you."

I asked, "What did I say that was mean?"

Alicia pouted, "Dry the dishes." She had washed the dishes, and I had rinsed the dishes. I had cooked the meal and stood watch on deck.

June 16th

Dear Dick and Mary, We spent yesterday and this morning at Split, Yugoslavia. We're now at the other end of Bay of Castles. The bridge doesn't lift anymore so tomorrow we'll have to return back. I've enjoyed Yugoslavia with the spectacular evergreen trees on the mountains, and the interesting old villages. Food is expensive here. It's a nuisance when our anchor drags and breaks loose when we're eating breakfast. The children and I miss the good old USA, people who speak English, a washing machine and running fresh water. Most of all, we miss our dear friends. Love you, Elsie

June 18th

At seven in the morning, an old woman rowed her dinghy right in front of our yacht. I had to divert our course.

Alan heard porpoises making sounds while he was still in the forward cabin. He came out and told us. There was a school of porpoises swimming and diving around us. It was good weather today. Alan had Sunday school for Alicia and himself. We moored out in the harbor at Palostane (a small village) for the night and ran aground in the morning.

June 19th

The family took a dip in the ocean to bath. At two in the morning, our yacht careened and we were high and dry. By seven in the morning, we leveled off, but still needed a couple more feet of sea water before we could sail.

June 21st 1978

Dear Connie, I feel responsible to try to keep our family together and out of danger in spite of living on a sloop-rigged yacht. I'm helpless, abandoned and torn from a sensible life. Safety has to be a twenty-four hour, every day issue. I never dreamt I'd be writing you from a communist country. Nor that we'd be sailing past Albania as we did with utmost care on June 7th and 8th. I'm nearly out of tracts – send me some please.

Greece was flooded with communist posters and propaganda. We're working our way up the Yugoslavian coast to Venice, Italy.

Thank Marilyn Clay, Bette Barre, and Diane Brown for praying for our family. As of April, a miracle happened. Alan hasn't been seasick anymore! At last! We left Cyprus which is south of Turkey and have anchored in little "Harbor of Saint Paul" in Lindos, Rhodes. It seemed so great to moor our yacht in the harbor and take our dinghy to shore where Paul landed. I sang songs to our Lord from the mountain.

I surely do miss my friends and church fellowship. We'll be in the Canaries next October and cross the Atlantic for the second time in mid-November. Love, Elsie

Left Preko and went several miles when we were hit by a hard northwest wind and heavy rain. We hove to and then motored to a small bay. Our anchor dragged during a "Bora" when local men came out in their boat to tell us to come in closer to the harbor. The best helper was Govio Hikoa, who spoke some English and was working a scuba boat, *Brod 25*. He helped us tie up in the harbor. Our yacht sat on the bottom during the night as the tide was out. The town was Ugljan. Jim declared, "I'm going into town to the local hotel to get information. You and the kids stay here."

June 22nd

We sailed to a tiny port of Zapuntel and anchored down at 6:30 P.M. Our family went ashore for dinner, which consisted of a cabbage and radish salad with vinegar and oil dressing, hamburger patties, mashed potatoes, plus lemon cake for dessert. A local man reported, "There are tiny jellyfish in this harbor. Have your children be careful."

The next morning Alan boasted, "Look what I caught!" He held up a pail with a small, brown, lace-like jellyfish in it.

Jim ordered, "Get rid of that now! Don't go back in this water! You could get stung."

June 25th

Sailed past Brioni Islands – a Navy ship circled close in front of us. A sailor motioned for us to go further out from shore and to continue on. Jim related, "Tito's summer residence is here."

June 26th

Jim decided, "Will check out of Yugoslavia this morning and head for Venice. It's about one hundred miles away."

Feelings of loneliness overwhelmed me. Our dirty yacht … no baths … dirty clothes … no fellowship with believers. I carried a heavy load of groceries as I walked back from the village "This is wearing me down, it's not a vacation. It's a hardship. I can't take this anymore!" I lost my temper. Before we left California, I had read Arthur Wallis's book on the baptism in the Holy Spirit which I tossed in the garbage. Satan really has been deceiving me on *this gift*! God ministered to me as I prayed.

June 27th

6 A.M. We approached Venice, Italy. Jim shouted, "Watch out! There are three cyclones ahead!" One cyclone swirled above the water surface on the port side and two cyclones were in the sky on our starboard side. We motored in and tied up at "Porto Turistico Veneziano" close to very elaborate buildings. Alan grinned, "Wow, shiny black gondolas – neat! " We walked for thirty minutes to Saint Mark's Square. The cathedral is like something out of *Grim's Fairy Tales*. We toured the Doge's Palace and then rode the ferry down the Grand Canal.

June 30th

We walked all the way to the Ponte Rialto. Small bridges abounded over the waterways. Alan was excited. "I met a 12 year old boy from New York. He told me that it only took seven hours to fly here." Alan and Alicia needed friends.

July 2nd

Our family attended the Biennale D'Arte 1978 where the theme was "From Nature to Art, from Art to Nature". I preferred Australia's and Romania's entries the best.

July 4th

We left Venice and motored to a small harbor in Chioggia, Italy. We rowed ashore in our dinghy to buy groceries. Jim, Alan and Alicia, walked around the village. I bought groceries and strolled back to our dinghy. As I leaned over to put the groceries and my purse in the dinghy, my foot slipped and I fell off the dock into the murky canal water. My purse and the groceries were safe and dry in the small dinghy. I was soaked from my neck to the bottom of my shoes. My hands gripped the edge of a corrugated metal sheet that held back the dirt bank. I struggled to lift myself up. I didn't have the physical strength to do this. I cried, "Help! Someone … I can't hang on to the side of this canal much longer."

A short distance away, I saw an Italian fisherman on a commercial fishing boat. He sat in the stern of his boat as he fiddled with a large fishing net. I tried over and over again to pull myself up and over the muddy bank and the metal sheet that reinforced the canal's edge. In desperation I continued to shout, "Help! Help! Please help me get out of the canal. Do you understand English?"

The fisherman still ignored me. A truck sped around the corner and stopped suddenly. Two young Italian truck drivers jumped out of the truck, rushed to me, and pulled me out of the canal. Water poured off my clothes and out of my shoes.

"Thank you. Tante grazie. Molto bene grazie." I panted the words out as I caught my breath. That was all the Italian I could remember.

My favorite soft pink slack suit was ruined, soiled with muddy salt water. The men didn't say a word, but rushed back to their truck. They jumped in and drove off. I trembled from exhaustion. What if they hadn't stopped? I would have drowned since my energy was drained. I could not hold on any longer.

I was ready to try to get back into our dinghy again when Jim and the kids showed up. Jim asked, "Did you trip? You're a mess!"

Alan questioned me, "Mom, how'd you get so full of mud and water? You'd yell at us if we did that."

I explained what happened as I pointed to the fisherman. "He wouldn't help me. Maybe he's deaf? You'd think he'd see me struggling in the water. I couldn't pull myself out of the canal. My arms aren't strong enough. The metal sheet was slippery."

Alan asked, "How did you get out?"

"Two truck drivers, or maybe they were angels, came driving around that corner. They saw me, stopped their truck, ran over here and pulled me out. I would've drowned."

Alan exclaimed, "Wow. Awesome."

Jim retorted, "Next time leave more of the painter out so the dinghy won't pull away from the edge. Let's go home and have dinner." We returned to our yacht. I know my rescuers were sent from God.

July 8th

Anchored in Losing (in front of Alhambra) where Jim and Alan skin-dived to check the propeller and shaft. A plastic bag and lots of nylon line were around the prop and shaft.

July 19th

It was late morning when we arrived near the foot of Italy in the middle of an Italian harbor. Jim tried several times to set the Danforth anchor at our bow, and our CQR anchor at our stern. It was a muddy harbor. He announced, "I'm going ashore."

My heart cringed, "*Please* don't, Jim. I'm uneasy about your going ashore when you've had so much trouble setting the anchors. We want to get on land too."

He insisted, "You'll be fine. I have to go ashore."

I muttered, "Meanwhile the kids and I are stuck out here on the yacht."

In the afternoon, I scribbled notes on paper with this heading: "How to be Creative in a Galley". The wind increased and the waves grew larger. Alan yelled, "Mom, we're drifting out. Help!"

I dropped my pencil when I heard Alan's cry for help. I dashed out of the main cabin, up the companionway and out into the cockpit. Our yacht was drifting out with the outgoing tide. Alan tried to reset an anchor. The anchor didn't catch. I ordered, "Get life jackets on at once. Run up the family flag! Your dad needs to see this from shore. He knows it means to return to our yacht at once."

Alan jumped into the main cabin and got the four foot by three foot family flag. He ran up the steps, hopped into the cockpit, climbed the starboard shroud and mounted the flag. Our yacht was being blown closer to the harbor exit.

The children and I waved our arms at other cruising people on their yachts in the harbor. We shouted, "Help us, our yacht is being pulled out to sea by the tide. Our anchors aren't holding. The captain is ashore. He hasn't seen that we are in trouble."

Two young men in their early twenties, dove off the stern of their yacht, and swam rapidly to *Far Horizons*. Alan put the swim ladder over the side of our yacht. He held out the overboard rescue pole for the men to grab. Alan instructed, "Alicia, get the life rings. Be ready to toss them to the men, but only if I tell you."

Alicia obeyed and held onto the life rings. The two men, Maynor and Brino, climbed aboard our yacht. Immediately, they took charge of pulling in the ineffective anchors. They started our inboard diesel engine to reposition our yacht back into the harbor. Maynor and Brino reset both anchors. Brino asked, "Where is the captain? You were so close to being pulled out to sea by the tide."

I responded, "My husband is ashore. When my son saw that the anchors had broken loose, he put up our family flag. Thank you both so much for rescuing us."

Maynor replied, "We're glad to help."

Alan praised, "You're super. Thanks for being so great and helping us.

Alicia spoke, "I want to thank you, too."

A third man, Hans, motored over in a dinghy and picked up Maynor and Brino. He took them back to their yacht.

An hour later, Jim pulled alongside *Far Horizons* in the hard dinghy. He fumbled with the painter, killed the outboard motor and stumbled aboard.

I questioned, "Didn't you see our family flag? The anchors didn't hold in the mud. Our yacht started drifting out with the current toward the opening in the harbor. The children and I were petrified."

Jim rationalized, "I had a few beers, got talking, didn't notice the time. Forgot to look at the yacht."

Alan reported, "Dad, two great men dove off their stern and swam over to rescue us. They reset our anchors after getting us back into the center of the harbor."

Alicia sulked, "Daddy, I was afraid. I called and called for you to come home. You didn't answer me."

Jim checked our position and the anchors. He wiped his chin and mumbled, "Going to sleep. Things look settled. We'll talk about it tomorrow."

The anchors had to be reset twice more during the night. This was a terrible harbor. Other yachts drifted loose.

July 20th

Our anchor got snagged with anchors from other boats. Jim snorkeled to free our anchor. A strong north wind sent huge waves. We made it to Santa Maria de Leluca and anchored.

July 21st

Jim fixed the exhaust. What a messy job. Winds were high for several days, so we were unable to make headway.

July 24th

Alicia started to sing a song: "Oh, can it be. I've found the secret to know you. I am weak but you are strong. I can never forget … you came to earth and died on the cross for our sins." She took a deep breath and looked into the sky. "You've given me strength to cross the Atlantic. You have more strength than I need. You can give me, Lord, what I need to get back to America." She stopped singing. We marveled at the littlest member of our family being so strong.

July 25th

After breakfast, I gathered the children around the table. "Today, let's talk about three things God is. He is love. He is our protector and he is our provider."

Alan suggested, "We need to thank him for loving us, protecting us, and for giving us food and clothing."

Alicia prompted, "And for this home on a sailboat, and for Daddy."

I answered, "Very good, children. You're right." This journey tried their hearts.

July 27th

We attempted to leave Milazzo at six in the morning. As we motored to the Lipari Islands, we saw our first volcano high and barren with small scrubby vegetation. We passed other islands between columns of rock that projected out of the seawater. We made it to Salinas Island and anchored. We could see "Stromboli" volcano at night even though it was forty miles distant. It was very impressive but it is not active. We could see red fire with reddish-gray smoke.

July 29th

We left Filicudi in the Aeolian Islands, Sicily and motored to Alicundi and anchored. The children swam ashore. This was a fishing village and a volcanic island. I recounted,

"Alan and Alicia, last night I saw a falling star and then a meteor – possibly a fireball. It was three times the length of the falling star."

Our food supplies were limited. I fixed rice and coleslaw for dinner last night.

I mused, "I'll try this casserole today: sea shell noodles, one can spinach, one can of corn, and one can of tuna. This I can sprinkle with basil, oregano, onion salt, and cheese. We haven't seen white sugar, confectionary sugar, or boullion for many ports. Jim, we need fresh milk and juice for the children; canned fruit, vegetables and packaged cheese. There are only five cans of fruit left."

Chapter 15

Onward and Forward

July 31st

M ondello Lido, Sicily was crowded with tourists. It was a hot day. I was bitten six times on my left arm during the night. We stocked up on groceries while our children played. Jim reported, "There's a south wind, so we'll leave for Sardinia tomorrow at six in the morning."

August 1st
Once we were out of Sicily the seas got rough. We observed packs of blunt nose whales squealing and swimming all about us for an hour and a half. A great wind pushed us along all day and night. It was a dark night and the air was heavy.

August 2nd
There was a downwind at 1:30 P.M. so Captain Jim announced, "The northeast wind has changed my decision. We'll bypass Sardinia and go on to Majorca." Our little family took salt water sponge baths. It felt great. Two large

vessels were spotted in the last twenty-four hours. I started my alfalfa garden.

We were on a broad reach and still hadn't seen Sardinia. Alan cut his finger with the bread knife. At 6:45 P.M. we anchored near Pula, Sardinia on the south tip of Sardinia.

August 3ʳᵈ

The seas were sloppy with a nice wind all the way to Carloforte where Jim tied our yacht with the bow facing the sea wall. We met Loggie, Sue, Maurita, and George plus our children found two new friends, Rolf and Kim from England and Finland. We enjoyed the time spent together.

August 5ᵗʰ

I traded two cans of beef for three pairs of scissors to be sharpened. Jim traded cruising books for a wind ventimeter.

August 6ᵗʰ

We woke up at 6:30 A.M. when Jim tried to motor out of the Carloforte harbor. The yacht ran aground twice. Alicia made a picture to give to George, Maurita, Rolf and Kim. She also gave them her little white New Testament. I said, "Alicia, you have such love for people." There was a nice southeast wind the rest of the day. The barometer dropped in the late evening.

August 7ᵗʰ

Today was a horrible day and night with high seas and wind 32 mph. We laid ahull from 7:25 P.M. to midnight. Jib put up at midnight. Alan vomited once.

August 8ᵗʰ

We experienced rain squalls and very high waves as we motored into Menorca at Mahon. We rafted up to *Mar y Paz* and enjoyed seeing Kermit and Dolores again. Kermit said, "We plan to cross the Atlantic also this year."

August 9th

Dolores, Alan, Alicia and I went into town to get food. The produce was good and reasonable. When we got back, Jim offered, "Elsie, let's go to a movie tonight. Midnight Cowboy is playing in English." Of course I jumped at this chance.

We came in contact with Colin and Brenda (a yoga teacher) on their yacht, *La Jonquil* from Channel Islands, New Jersey. Jim asked, "How was your trip? Did you see the yacht, *Alk* from Holland?" We wanted to hear of our other cruising friends.

August 10th

We connected with Vann and Chuck on *Quest* to compare notes and reports on sea routes. He revealed, "I'm a lawyer from Corona. I write books and have three grown children. What's your next port?"

August 12th

We sailed from Mahon along the south coast of Menorca. The waters were a beautiful aqua color. We arrived in Ciudadela and rafted up with *Mar y Paz* again. Alan wrote his poems. Kermit invited us over for dinner. I rejoiced, "Praise you, Lord Jesus!" Later Dolores came over to our yacht to share. We have become great friends.

August 13th

We departed Cuidadela and sailed to Port Saller. Alan helmed us in for the first time and did fine. Pears were a good bargain in Mallorca. Genene Kearns called, "Hey, MacGregors, remember when we met you in Chalan, France? We docked today. Come over for a visit." Their yacht, *Elephant Rock*, was helmed by her husband, Gordon. We exchanged news of fellow cruisers and traded books. Genene gave Alan and Alicia a can of popcorn.

August 14th

We anchored off the island of Majorca. Our kids dove off the yacht and swam around it. They splashed each other and laughed as I watched them. Jim left for the island in the morning to look for a tool to repair the engine. I mentioned, "When near shore, watch out for sea urchins. They're black spiny sea creatures. If you step on one, it's very painful. I was told to use meat tenderizer on the skin to loosen and pull the spine out."

Alicia asked, "Do they look like porcupines?"

I replied, "Yes, except they are round and much smaller."

In the evening, Jim returned with sea urchins he'd purchased from a shore vendor. I quizzed, "I was telling the kids earlier to watch out for them. I described what they looked like so they would be careful. How are they prepared?"

Jim demonstrated, "Easy. Watch. I'm going to cut the sea urchin in half like this. Whack!" The knife cut the shell in half. Black gooey stuff poured out on the counter.

I shuddered, "What's that black stuff?"

Jim explained, "The inside of the sea urchin. Now throw out the black stuff, wash what's left and put the shell in a serving bowl.

I agreed, "I can do that." I first rinsed the sea urchins inside and out with sea water, then with fresh water. "Then what?"

Alicia wondered, "Do you cook the sea urchins?"

Jim instructed, "No, when you're ready to eat, take a small piece of bread and scoop out the small pieces of pink meat."

I asked, "Alicia, please set the table while I make the noodles and vegetables. Be sure to put the bread and butter on because we'll need the bread to scoop out the small pieces of pink meat."

Alicia bounced off the side berth. "Okay, Mommy." She set the table. Suddenly, she squealed, "They're trying to get out of the dish!" Half of a sea urchin crawled over the top edge of the bowl.

I blurted, "Don't tell Alan. He's a finicky eater as you know."

Alicia answered, "Okay, I won't tell."

Our family sat down at the table to eat dinner. Alan avoided touching the urchins. He refused to try even one little piece. Alicia and I did our best to keep from bursting out in laughter.

Jim insisted, "Alan, take a small piece of bread and scoop out the pink meat with it. Then eat it."

Alicia instigated, "Alan, fish eyes are my favorite. They taste like bubble gum."

Alan retorted, "Ick. You have the worst sense of food. You're disgusting."

When we anchored out off another small island, I gave Jim and Alan a large plastic bowl with a lid, a grocery list, plus money sealed inside the bowl, and a yellow plastic egg carton that held a dozen eggs. I said, "Go and get some groceries."

Jim said, "Alan, let's swim to shore." They pushed the plastic containers in front of them.

Later, Alicia said, "Mom, here comes Alan. He's halfway to our yacht. He's pushing the egg carton."

I added, "I see your Dad swimming toward us with the bowl floating on top of the water. Let's see if he bought some food."

Jim and Alan climbed aboard to show their success at a new version of buying food. Jim took the lid off the bowl. With a sweep of one hand, he produced his treasures one by one. He declared, "Onions, mozzarella cheese, Italian dark olives - delicious ... 'cause I ate some - two lemons, and change in the bowl."

I giggled, "And they're all dry. Good job, you two."

Alan boasted, "Look, Mom. The eggs aren't broken."

I smiled, "I'm bursting with pride over you."

August 23rd

Dozens of ships were sighted since yesterday. We'd covered forty-six miles by 4:15 A.M. Jim turned the motor on at 6 A.M. as the sun came up. *Far Horizons* arrived in Alicante, Spain at three in the afternoon. *Mar y Paz* was docked two boats away from us.

August 24th

Our water tanks were filled. I washed clothes and blankets in buckets on deck as usual. Alicante had the largest market we'd ever seen. Jim commented, "There are two large floors with meats, fish, eggs, cheese, flowers, and bread. I heard that the other building has vegetables, good potatoes, and fruit. We'll need to make two trips in order to carry enough food back to our yacht."

I shared, "I tried a new fruit today – higos chumbos. It's from a desert cactus. It's very sweet. Cut off the ends, peel the skin off, and eat the pulp and seeds. Try it."

Jim smacked his lips, "A feast tonight. We stocked up enough food for weeks except for eating the fresh meat tonight."

Alicante's sidewalks were very decorative. They displayed a wavy pattern in blue, white, and red design. The boulevard was lined with palm trees. We walked past a large beach and then up an elevator to see Castile Santa Barbara. What a position and a view in all directions. It appears untakeable. Muy caliente dia!

August 25th

Jim filled all propane tanks. We encountered Diane and Alan on their yacht, *Casper*. They have two sons, Steven and Julian, so we gave them our pre-primer books.

At 2 P.M. we departed Alicante with a fair wind and sailed all night. A Spanish naval vessel accompanied a large speed boat that followed the Spanish coastline.

Jim pondered, "Wonder who's in the speed boat? Who's so important to be accompanied by a naval vessel?" We noticed this vessel in the distance for two days.

August 28th

We docked at Club Nautico de Motril at 1:45 P.M. in Motril, Spain. We took a bus into Motril for groceries and a chunk of ice. At 8:15 P.M. I walked around the dock in the marina when I heard Spanish people as they called, "El Rey! El Rey! El Rey!"

I asked, "What does 'El Rey' mean?"

A yachtsman replied, "It means The King." The large speed boat and the Spanish naval vessel entered the harbor of Motril. I rushed closer to the dock as the king arrived.

The tall, handsome king walked down the dock. He wore a short-sleeved, dark blue T-shirt with his yacht's name *Fortuna*, and khaki shorts. A crowd of Spanish people tried to get close to him. I held my hand out over the shoulders of some people. King Juan Carlos turned his head, saw me and took my hand. I said, "God bless you." I then snapped a photo of him.

A lady cried, "Look there's the Queen of Spain in the pink gown, and another royal person wearing the green gown." The people presented a bouquet of flowers to each person. The royal party left the marina via black limosines which sped out of the marina entrance. Villagers waved as they stood outside the marina walls.

I returned to our yacht. Jim ordered, "I want you to sand the teak rail."

I looked down at my hand and with a look of wonderment replied, "Oh, no, this hand just shook the hand of the King of Spain. You want me to do what? I'm not going to wash it. I am honored to have met him." Alan and Alicia stood with open mouths as they looked at me in amazement. Jim didn't say another word.

August 30th

We left Motril at 8 A.M. and at 11 A.M. a school of porpoises chased tuna. Alan made grilled cheese sandwiches for everyone. They were perfect. Then the family got sick with high temperatures and diarrhea for several days.

September 3rd

We tied up at Gibraltar at 6 P.M. We saw Joe and Sandy Moyer on *Destiny,* whom we had met one and a half years ago in Antigua in the West Indies. Jim and I got mail that his stepfather, Bill, had died in a car accident last July 30th.

September 5th

I met Marilyn Heavens, Ruth, and Sheila Patron in a Bible Book Store. Marilyn invited me to her houseboat, *Hamarr,* for prayer and fellowship. She spoke in tongues. I had been filled with unbelief and doubt regarding speaking in tongues when I left the United States. The church I attended did not approve of tongues. The lonely night watches and severe storms drew me in a closer relationship with the Lord. I trusted him for guidance.

September 6th and 7th

Jim's birthday was the day before mine. I was very sick and weak. Marilyn Heavens came over and prayed for me. I can sense the beauty of the Lord in Marilyn. "Elsie, this is a birthday gift for you." She handed me a book, *In the Arena*, by Isobel Kuhn. We met Phyllis and Roland Cooper. We had a lovely dinner at Paddington's Restaurant where Jim had Paddington's Toredors, and I had Steak Diana.

One afternoon, I visited Marilyn. I felt devastated and beat up emotionally. I could not lift my head. I felt a heavy weight on my head, shoulders, and arms. She prayed for me in tongues. Then she played a song, "You're my Glory and the Lifter of my Head." She played it again. The Lord began to encourage me and gradually, I was able to finally raise my head. The weight lifted off me. I sensed a new freedom.

September 9th

Mar y Paz arrived. I gave Kermit and Dolores a book, *The Hiding Place*. I went to see Pastor Cooper and his wife. He pastored Bethel Tabernacle. They drove us to the beach to see the red and white striped lighthouse. Phyllis offered, "You may wash clothes at our apartment."

September 11th

Pastor Cooper gave our family a tour of Gibraltar. As we entered St. Michael's Cave, the song "Amazing Grace" permeated the gigantic cave. I was in awe, "These are the most beautiful stalagtites and stalagmites I've ever seen." I was filled with praise for the Lord.

A Barbary ape, the size of a large toddler, jumped on Jim's back when we were outside. Jim bent over as he tried shaking the ape off.

September 9th

Alan told me, "Mom, I prayed last night that if God wanted us to stay, that he'd send a sign." A thick fog rolled in this morning. Alan said, "That's the sign."

September 14th

We set out for Algeciras to a stinky harbor where the customs persons were touchy. Jim decided to sail back to Gibraltar the next morning. We got a hot bath in a public bath place for thirty cents each.

September 17th

Sailed wing on wing from Gibraltar and arrived in the fishing village, Barbate. *Caravel* rafted up to us. Kitty and Fred shared the evening with us. The next morning, Jim reported, "Our gear shift has broken. I'll try to fix it at sea." It was a slow trip and got rough off Cape Trafalgar. He did fix the gear shift.

We rafted up at Puerto de Santa Maria to *Venus*, a Swiss yacht where we came in contact with Armando. We linked with Earnest and Jan from Holland on their yacht, *R. C. Takebora*. Puerto de Santa Maria is situated on banks of the Guadalete River in the province of Cadiz, Spain. Jim instructed, "Columbus sailed from here on his second voyage to the Americas."

When tied up in Santa Maria, I asked God to baptize me in the Holy Spirit. .

September 21st

I read, "I know that Jesus' Holy Spirit is guiding me into everything that is true." (John 16:13) Found a note of mine from 8/12/78 in Phillip's Translation of Acts 1:5 "*Before many days are passed you will baptized with the Holy Spirit.*" Discovered another note dated 8/30/78: "*They were living as simply men and women who had been baptized in the name of the Lord Jesus. So then and there they laid their hands on them and they received the Holy Spirit.*"

September 22nd

Jim was ill with a high fever for several days. I spoke one word about 10 P.M. – "Nah-talk-ah". I felt like a baby learning to talk. No feeling, spoke another word ... did I give myself that one? Doubt flooded my thoughts. There were no Christians to talk with. I was so frustrated, confused, and lonely.

September 23rd

I walked a long way to town and scraped my back as I crawled under a fence on a bridge which tore a hole in my blouse. On the way back, I scraped my arm. I gave two tracts to Maria Bartolome who lives in Colon, and another to a begging man with one leg. Maria has grey short hair, and is well-dressed.

Jim bought four new Spanish fenders for our yacht. He said, "Alan, help me put new lines on the fenders."

Alicia snapped, "At last I get proper fenders so I can do my job right. The ones we had were flat in the middle."

Jim and Alan went to the bullfights in Santa Maria. Alan shared, "Mom, it was great.

Bloody for the bulls and the matadors got chased."

While they were gone, I wrote five letters. I read most of *One in the Spirit* by David Watson.

September 24th

Jim and Alan fixed lines on the new fenders. I washed clothes. They dried quickly on this hot day.

September 25th

We've been here a week. I've begun reading *In the Arena* by Isabel Kuhn.

September 26th – 27th

We left Santa Maria and sailed to the beginning of the Guadalquier River. It was dirty, and muddy water all the way. We sailed with our genoa up part of the way and passed a native village with thatched roofs on dry, flat land. There were very few trees. We motored through one lock and there was "Seville". At 7:30 P.M. we tied up to a rickety dock.

September 28th – 29th

Jim and I walked into Seville among beautiful old buildings, a large park and to a cathedral that indicated Christopher Columbus's body was buried there. After 9 P.M. a boy threw rocks at our yacht. Jim shouted, "Policia! Policia!" He shined a light on the boy who fled.

September 30th

We toured Alcazar with Moorish architecture, beautiful tapestries, coaches, lovely gardens, and also the naval museum, Tower of Gold. The next morning we attempted to leave Seville at 8 A.M. The lock was closed until 5 P.M., so we had to return to the old dock. About 5:30 P.M. the boathook went overboard and sank. Jim's temper flared. I mused, "Ah, the better or for worse."

We heeled to port during the night and ran aground. Jim coughed, "I'm getting a cold. It felt like standing up while trying to sleep." Our crew had grown weary.

At last we got back to Santa Maria. On the way in, I banged the top of my head on a ferry exit. I groaned, "The pain is shooting down into my neck!" On the way home, the toe of my left shoe got caught in a rope tied to a spare tire at the ferry dock. I tripped (at a run) when two dozen eggs flew out of my handbag. I injured my right hand and knee as I fell. I picked myself up and reported, "Jim, it was a battle today getting places. One good thing happened though, I rescued ten eggs. What a day!"

We were able to find a sweet powdered milk called "Molica" (made in Swisa) which dissolved instantly and tasted good. Jim spoke, "I heard that we can get milk that is made up and keeps for months without refrigeration. It's called Ram."

October 4th

My body is still sore and stiff today after the incidents at the ferry. We left Spain at the Cadiz exit in the morning. Jim decided, "I'm setting our course toward Madeira which is a Portuguese island about three hundred sixty miles west of Morocco." The northwest wind filled our sails on this sunny day. At 2:30 P.M. the wind died. Jim started our diesel engine.

In the distance a patrol boat headed straight for us at a high speed. It pulled alongside our yacht. A Spanish patrol boat officer, in a naval uniform, asked, "Where are you going? You'll have to change course!"

Jim answered, "Headed toward Madeira."

The patrol boat officer ordered, "Change course to north or northwest at three hundred thirty degrees. Now!"

Jim challenged, "That's quite a change. We're headed at two hundred thirty degrees."

The officer warned, "You are on a collision course with a Spanish Naval target ship. Move out!" Jim swung the helm to change course north. A target ship passed in the near distance in front of *Far Horizons*.

Jim shrank, "Oh, no, there's the target sleeve. When we had target practice in the U.S. Navy, we didn't do that good at hitting the target." Shots were heard as firing commenced toward the target sleeve. We could see large puffs of black smoke from our deck. Our family stared in unbelief and shock. Jim gasped, "Whew that was pretty close."

Alan asked, "Dad, are we going to be shot?"

Jim's brow furrowed, "I hope not." No notice of this target practice had been given.

A radio operator on an English commercial vessel was heard on our radio. He yelled, "I'm furious! Why weren't we notified of this target practice? I'm reporting this to your government. You will be reprimanded!"

Chapter 16

Perilous Progress

Jim turned, "Elsie, kids, we've lost our chance to get to Madeira. It'll take longer, but the next landfall has to be the Canary Islands."

October 7th

We had been motoring for three days, when at 1 o'clock in the morning, the diesel motor quit. A strange vessel seemed to be following us. Jim changed our course several times. The pursuing vessel stayed on our path. Jim called on VHF 16, "Ship ahoy. Why are you following us?" No answer. Jim turned off the running lights and all cabin lights. The moon was covered with clouds. The motor wouldn't start. The vessel kept on our heading. Jim raised the sails. A strong breeze picked up and Jim changed our course again. Jim threatened, "I have a gun. Lay off. I repeat … do not follow us."

Jim altered our course. He took out his shotgun. Jim was visibly shaken. The kids and I were terrified. We held each other. Alan asked, "Do they still see us?"

I responded, "Alan and Alicia, you both have done such good jobs. Yes, you're both blue water sailors. I'm so proud of you."

Alicia shivered, "Why is Daddy scared?" She started to cry. *Far Horizons* changed direction and lost the motor vessel in the dark about 3:15 in the morning. A nice wind blew the rest of the night. Jim fixed the motor.

October 7th – 8th

A strong wind blew so we used a reefed main and working jib. Both of our children were under the weather. I prayed that Alicia would be able to eat. We lay ahull from noon to 5 P.M. I complained, "This isn't the way to travel."

October 10th – 11th

Lightning and heavy storms obscured the sky so Jim couldn't use his sextant to check our position. I held my hand over my stomach. My other hand braced my head as I weaved from side-to-side. The noise of the waves pounded against the hull. Alan asked, "Mom, what's wrong? Are you seasick?"

I moaned, "I'll be okay. It must be the fumes from the diesel fuel. Thanks for checking."

October 12th

This was our eighth day out at sea since we left Spain. Alan and I learned Psalm 117. Alan's reward was the book *Voyages of Dr. Doolittle*. After breakfast the kids were given reading lessons in their workbooks.

October 14th

A good position report via *Baron*, a Monrovian-Iberian ship told us that we were 125 to 130 miles from the Canaries. This was our eleventh day at sea.

October 16th

We arrived at 10 A.M. in Arrecife, Lanzarote in the Canary Islands. We rafted next to *Foreign Affair*. This was a dirty harbor. After buying food supplies in town, we moved to a cleaner anchorage, Palermo. Alan learned Psalm 134. His reward was *Dr. Doolittle's Office*.

October 17th

Alan's dinghy, *Swallow* was launched. He decided to be Captain Flint. He had made a brown square cloth sail, and used an adjustable centerboard that hung over the side of the dinghy. He announced, "It works great." His first guest was Captain Jim MacGregor who came aboard at 9:30 A.M.

I complained, "Jim, this has been a terrible afternoon. The gear broke again, the port lifeline broke, and water squirts on my legs when I pump the toilet. There's no time alone; my back and fingers hurt, no privacy, and there are high winds. I must have strained my right chest and back muscles carrying heavy groceries two days ago. I feel like a pack mule."

October 22nd

Jim ordered, "Kids, we're going to get fresh food. We'll be back as fast as we can. Stay on the yacht. There's a strong current in this harbor."

Alan replied, "Okay, Dad, hurry back." Jim and I got in the Avon raft, motored to shore and tied it up,

Jim and I carried bags of groceries to the harbor. Jim shouted, "What! Elsie! There's Alan and Alicia rowing the dinghy near the rock break wall! How did they get to shore? Kids! Oh, God, they could have been blown out to sea." We dropped our groceries, rushed over to our children and hugged them. Jim uttered, "Don't you ever do a stunt like this again. We were coming right back."

After lunch, a discussion ensued. Alan confessed, "I buried a treasure and now I can't find it. I got so excited when the dink blew away that I've forgotten where I buried it."

Alicia piped up, "What was it? I'll help you find it."

Alan retorted, "I'm not telling. It's a secret."

November 5th

We sailed into Las Palmas, Gran Canary and moved into the inner harbor due to choppy seas and heavy wind. The following day we met Dolores Wall at the El Corte Ingles, a six story building with reasonable prices and most everything one might need.

November 9th

We departed Las Palmas at 4 A.M. with a north wind. We had a beautiful sail. Jim talked with Sam Geiger on *Rights of Man* VHF radio. We arrived in Puerto Rico on the Gran Canaria about 2 P.M. when Barbara Geiger came over for a visit. We had met them on October 25th. David Geiger signed our guest book on October 30th and wrote: Shanghaied by *Far Horizons*.

November 12th

The children found a few friends from other cruising families. Alan bought a guitar from another yachtsman with the ten dollars he got for his birthday. He picked out some notes and taught himself to strum the guitar. He sang, "Oh, I'm a sailor man, sailing the seven seas ..."

Jim talked to a crusty-looking Australian sailor as he bragged about Alan. "My son's doing pretty good with that guitar. He likes math now. He used to hate school, maybe 'cause he was in the new bilingual program. He's written about five chapters on sea stories for boys."

November 13th

Jim boasted, "Elsie, I anticipate a victorious finale to our three years at sea. I can see the display of bright colors of the hand-sewn flags that you made, showing the countries we visited. You'll be glad that you gave in to me."

I didn't answer him. I moved toward the bow. I miss running fresh water, hot water, a bath tub, a toilet that just takes one pump instead of twenty pumps, a kitchen that stays level, ice cream, ice cubes, American products, a washing machine, privacy, and most of all – Christians!

November 14th

Our motor wouldn't start. Bengt Olausson from Sweden helped Jim work on our motor all day until 1 A.M. Two bolts had broken. The next morning we sailed to Pisada Blanco on a reefed main and jib, wing on wing. Swirly motion with moderate waves put us off on a good start. The barometer was very high at 1025 with a consistent steady wind.

November 17th

We've covered 240 miles. Jim used a Portugese fishing lure that Alan had traded two shark's teeth for (from Pete's Dad). Jim cast the line out, "I've got one." He fought and reeled the line in with a beautiful yellow turquoise Dorado fish about ten to fifteen pounds. The Dorado hit about ten seconds after Jim put the lure out. We feasted on the fresh fish.

November 18th

As of noon today, we've sailed 475 miles with 2700 total miles to cover for this second Atlantic passage crossing.

November 20th [P]

Our genoa ripped along the seam. Jim lowered the sail at 8 A.M. We fixed it with sailcloth and Bosdick 66. We put a reefed main and jib up. By noon we had covered 577 miles. Barometer dropped slowly and steadily the last two days. 1012 at 7 P.M.

Second garden started, eggs turned.

November 22nd

Jim had problems with the helm. We covered 714 miles by noon. It was a sweltering hot day. The 23rd was Thanksgiving Day when the trade winds started to push us over the waves. I exclaimed, "These trades are beautiful! Consistent! We're flying. Let's push on wing on wing."

November 24th

We've sailed 1192 miles by noon on the 26th. We had a rough evening and night. I was tossed out of bed in the main cabin. There is heavy rain and the seas are high.

November 27th

Jim said, "I'll finally be able to use my sextant and take the first sun shot on this passage. We've covered 1322 miles since we left the Canary Islands." At 3:45 P.M. Forced 7 gale winds – dropped the jib. Four more rain squalls. Alicia was thrown across the V-berth. A large wave splashed into our aft cabin during the night.

November 28th

Halfway across the Atlantic Ocean, Alan made a card for Jim. On the outside it read "Happy halfway across!" On the inside: "You should be proud, Captain. Aye that you should do, after getting halfway across the Atlantic Ocean; and taking us with you too."

Alan's card to me: On the outside – Cheer up mate, we're halfway across!

On the inside: You cook our breakfast, dinner and lunch, and I've a hunch we'll make it someday. So hold on mate, okay."

Jim announced, "We won't be going to the South Pacific, instead through Panama and up the Mexican coast to California."

Praise the Lord! I could barely believe his decision. The seas were still rough, but we were tracking well with just a jib. At noon – 1460 miles and time for our halfway party! Alan and Alicia were thrilled. Alan's gifts: toy horse and a Dr. Doolittle book. Alicia received a doll with a bathinette set, and games. Alicia gave me a shell.

November 29th

Eight flying fish had landed on deck. By noon we had reached 1598 miles out from the Canaries. Jim changed batteries and used the bilge pump to suck out sea water from the bilge. I decided, "I'm making homemade bread and pizza since I have some yeast left."

November 30th

I asked, "Jim, how much longer can we take this agitation? It's like being in a washing machine. Things always pitched about?" At noon 1733 miles attained.

December 1st 1978

Alan's pulse was only 58. He wasn't responding. We let him sleep later this morning. Clocks moved back an hour. At noon 1864 miles. The main dropped.

December 2nd

Alicia's growing in the Lord. She's reading the Bible. Both the children are participating in Sunday school. At noon 2002 miles.

December 3rd

The first propane tank is empty. Jim took sun shots for our position. He said, "We are over three-fourths of the way. Only six hundred more miles left to go! We tracked 155 miles today." Jim mentioned the possibility of settling in Florida. At 5 P.M. dozens of dolphins were swimming in different directions on both sides of our yacht. These were the most we'd ever seen at one time.

December 4th

Alicia is doing a word study on "love". She is reading the Scriptures to Alan and me. Today I claimed, "*And I will send an angel before thee ... unto a land flowing with milk and honey.*" Exodus 33:2-3 KJV and also "*... My presence shall go with you and I will give you rest.*" Exodus 33:14 KJV At noon – 2300 miles – hooray!

December 5th

Jim spotted a tanker (from Angola to Puerto Rico). The radio operator said, "I wish you a Merry Christmas and a Happy New Year!" There was a light rain and a double rainbow. At 8:30 P.M. we heard our first Christian radio station (called Radio Paradise) from St. Kitts. They played the song, "Winging My Way Back Home". Glory to God. That was right on target.

December 6th

There was a swift wind. Jim reported, "We should have only one more night at sea before we get to Barbados." At noon – 2569 miles.

December 7th

Land Ho! Barbados RDF picked up. It took us twenty-two days and 2707 miles to cross from the Canaries to Barbados! Alan exclaimed, "Wow, those are the cleanest white sand beaches!" We walked into Bridgetown and finally had a shower at the yacht club.

December 8th

A poem called "Wit's End Corner" caught my eye in a Christian Literature store. It spoke to my heart and soul. Jim went ashore and capsized the dinghy. I met Godfrey O'Neale and Richard Garnes, two Christians. Richard invited me to his church, People's Cathedral. Godfrey traveled for Hospital Christian Fellowship International.

On December 10th children and I rode the bus to Pastor Richard's church. The church held two thousand people and it was full. Alicia and Alan attended Sunday school. Alicia used the microphone and said, "You must know the Lord. Then if you know the Lord, you should go to Sunday school."

I needed a ride to shore, so I prayed for a ride to shore. A Swede I'd met in Puerto Rico Marina in Gran Canary came rowing by, so I was able to get to the evening service.

December 11th

Jim exploded with jealousy so he threw a flashlight and a bucket at me. He always wanted to be the center of attention. He yelled, "Shut up!"

I went to the head and cried, "Jesus, you are the Victor in this situation. Satan, you cannot have Jim's soul!" Without the Lord and my heavenly Father, I would never have been able to make this journey.

Chapter 17

West Indies Incidents

December 12th

We tied a line from our bow to a tree ashore at Admiralty Bay, Bequia and Jim set out a stern anchor. This eased our yacht from most of the wave action. This was a green, hilly island with palm trees and a calm harbor. We all had a peaceful sleep. Before Jim changed the channel on the radio, we heard "If you're seeking peace – The Man of Peace is calling you."

December 14th

We bought nice potatoes and frozen chicken legs. I found a small Port Elizabeth Evangelical Church and met Inez Hazell who runs Cinderella Hide-Away with Ruth, her nine-year-old daughter. Inez's husband is Armond. I met Pastor Amos Dennis and his wife, Gloria. Later, I met Shawn at the meat shop. He said, "I read the tract you gave me yesterday and I said a prayer." I'll give him follow-up material tomorrow.

December 16th

Inez's daughter, Ruth, invited Jesus into her heart this morning. Glory to God! I was asked to teach the teenage class of about ten, and to speak in church. I gave my testimony and sang a song a cappella. The church didn't have any musical instruments. Gloria asked, "Elsie, when you leave our island, my one request is for you to send us a tambourine."

December 18th

Jim and Alan fixed new panels for the cupboard behind the rocking stove as a Christmas gift for me. Archie (Alan's friend) gave us a pumpkin, coconut and two limes. Alan slept in a hammock in front of our mast. The hammock was tied between two spreaders. Jim loves my Far Horizons Marinade: 1 c. ketchup, ½ c. brown sugar, 1/3 c. vinegar, lemon pepper, and one chalot (or onion). This is great on chicken or pork.

December 21st

Alan was very upset. He cried uncontrollably and felt ill. He sobbed, "Dad yells at me all the time." I tried to explain this to Jim. I think his heart is starting to soften. Pastor Dennis brought a cup of ice to the dock which was about twenty feet away. Alan went to get it and swam it back. Our first bit of ice in a long time. Alicia and Jim got more coconuts.

God gave me Hebrews 10:36, *"For ye have need of patience, that, ye have done the will of God, ye might receive the promise."*

I walked over to Amos Dennis's home. They have a refrigerator and ice, but no food in the refrigerator. They had beds, but only one sheet. I offered, "I have some sheets that I'd like to give you. Also some bars of soap." What one didn't have, the other did so we exchanged items and were blessed both ways. I felt so strengthened to have Christian fellowship.

Amos said, "I never told anyone that I didn't have any soap to wash, but one Sunday morning after church a woman handed me a small paper sack with one bar of soap in it. God knows our needs."

December 29th

Pastor Dennis and Gloria gave us a tour of Bequia in her volkswagon. Bequia is a special island with mountains, lovely flowers, and pigeon peas growing on trees. A lady believer in a vegetable market gave me four bananas. Gloria brought ice to us several times.

January 2nd 1979

We left Bequia and gave Stephanie a ride to Union Island. She traveled lightly with two small suitcases. Stephanie said, "I work six months and travel six months."

January 12th

Two propane tanks were filled. I bought thirty eggs and visited with Ann Carl on her yacht, *Audacious*.

January 14th

The tradewinds were back so we left Fort-de-France, Martinque to St. Pierre.

January 15th

We set sail from Martinique with a good wind, but choppy seas at 3:30 A.M. We anchored in Portsmouth, Dominica at 2:30 P.M. We were greeted by many boys selling fresh fruit from their small boats.

January 17th

We were unable to go up the Indian River as it was blocked by natives with their wooden dinghies. They said, "No fiberglass boats, no motors allowed." Alan and Alicia played with the children on shore. We were blocked by larger boats, this time behind and in front of the bridge on Indian River. Several young men threatened us.

January 18th 1979

Our yacht was anchored off the island of Dominica. Jim had gone ashore in our Avon raft. The children and I decided to go ashore in our fiberglass dinghy. We walked down a dirt road through a village of all black inhabitants. I turned my head to the left as my eyes focused upon a large wooden sign above a wooden shack with the words: I AM A BELIEVER. My heart leaped. A young black woman sat barefoot on the wooden steps. I called, "I am so glad to find a believer! My name is Elsie and these are my children, Alan and Alicia."

Her face lit up with a beautiful smile. She stood and held out her hand. "I'm Petrolina. Come into my home." We stepped into her barren shack. There wasn't any running water. No bathroom and in the backyard was a large washtub for bathing. The village had a general water faucet down the dirt road. She was twenty-two years of age and had two children; six-year-old girl and a two-year old son. We prayed together. On another day, the children and I paddled to shore with palm branches to pick up Petrolina. We brought her out to see our yacht. This was like seeing a statuesque princess. Clothes didn't matter. Her inner beauty glowed.

January 19th

I prayed, "This need in my spiritual life must be met soon. I need the fullness of the Holy Spirit – the overflowing. I cannot witness effectively to these different persons (Jews and oppressed) without the gift of tongues and the gift of

189

discernment. I need to be filled to overflowing with Jesus' resurrection power to carry out His work until He comes. I feel grieved because I do not have this gift. I feel it is a spiritual necessity. I do love the brethren of all races!"

1 Peter 2:6 *Wherefore also it is contained in the scripture, Behold, I lay in Sion a chief corner stone, elect, precious: and he that believeth on him shall not be confounded.* 1 Peter 2:6 (KJV)

January 20th

We need provisions badly. We are out of ketchup, brown sugar, canned fruit, canned vegetables, mayonnaise, coffee, toilet tissue, syrup, hard candy, Crisco, and oleo. I do have lots of bananas, grapefruit and canned tuna (from the Canary Islands).

Likewise, I say unto you, there is joy in the presence of the angels of God over one sinner that repenteth. Luke 15:10 (KJV)

January 23rd

Far Horizons sailed into English Harbor at Antigua. We had mail waiting for us. We went over to visit with Kermit and Dolores on their yacht, *Mar y Paz*. Mosquitoes are here and ready to feast on newcomers (we had been here in 1976).

We sailed on to different islands. Alicia picked a card from the promise box often. Today she picked one about love. She looked it up in her Bible, and marked it. She said, "That really fixed me up. I needed that."

January 28th

Jim was getting more thoughtful. He put up my clothesline last night ahead of time without being asked. He fixed the engine. I decided, "Today I'll wash our red and white striped curtains in the main cabin."

February 1st

Six people lost in Atlantic crossing: one French child, one Dutch man, and four single handers.

February 4th

Our gear shift gave way again as we left St. Bart's. Jim heard part of Billy Graham's message on the radio. Jim criticized, "He says the same thing he said twenty years ago."

I replied, "If a person doesn't act on the light he's been given, whether or not a Christian or a non-Christian; that person won't get any more new light." I spotted six ships on my watch.

February 5th

On our arrival in St. Croix the food left on our yacht as of today: one cup of rice, thirty-nine cans of tuna, two packages instant potatoes, ten pounds of flour, three cans of evaporated milk, six packages of noodles, one can of corned beef, five cans of tomato paste, one can of mackerel, one sugar icing, one sandwich spread, and four cans of pimentos.

February 8th

I mailed a new tambourine to Amos and Gloria Dennis in Bequia. Jim looked at part of a book titled *Know Why You Believe*. He said, "This guy ought to be locked up."

February 13th

I realized that God was restricting me to His will that I might know His glory. He'd put me in restrictive circumstances for this reason. I apologized to Jim and to the children for having a critical attitude at times. I requested the children's prayers for me about this.

February 14th

The head is fixed with new parts; new fiberglass coating put on dinghy.

February 17th

The Lord's clearing up my mind from old prejudices and ideas.

February 18th

We took on thirty gallons of diesel at St. Thomas and set off to Fajardo, Puerto Rico. The next day our water tanks were filled. Our family went over to visit the Taylors who had befriended us after our ordeal in the Bermuda Triangle in January 1977.

March 1st

Our anchor was weighed, and we motored to La Romana, Dominica Republic where we tied up for customs clearance. Our yacht was searched by two men. We saw trainloads of sugarcane pass over the bridge several times a day.

March 3rd

We headed west with a reefed main and jib under a strong east wind. The winds increased so Jim dropped the main and used a whisker pole for the jib. We covered 127 miles in 24 hours.

March 5th

Alan sleepwalked during the night. He headed for the companionway, picked up a chart, and stumbled around. I said, "Son, wake up. Turn around and go back to sleep in the side berth." I'm glad that I was on watch so he didn't come out into the cockpit.

March 7th

Jim took sun shots with the sextant to check our location as we sailed. Jim was not a believer. He had been resentful and resisting my faith in God for many years. For the past ten days, I have been singing a lament, a mournful song in the spirit. This wailing song blended in with the wind when I was on watch every night. I can't explain it, but I know that I was communicating with God. Truly, my spirit was speaking mysteries to God and pouring out the deepest cries of my heart. Was this a form of intercession? If so, who was it for?

Chapter 18

Portentous Voyage

It was ten o'clock in the evening, when Jim set our course toward the Panama Canal. The wind increased. He said, "We'd better reef the main and jib." Our yacht danced over the waves in the Caribbean Sea.

"Okay, it's your watch now, Elsie. I'm going to bed. Wake me in two hours."

The wind screeched as I took over the watch. My eyes searched the horizon in all directions for lights, ships or a shoreline. I checked the compass heading. The dark and empty horizon stared back.

Jim slept soundly in the aft cabin. Alicia and Alan nestled in their bunks. Alicia occupied the V-berth in the forward cabin. Alan settled in the main cabin's side berth.

I checked the compass heading every fifteen minutes. I spoke, "Lord, it'll be a relief when my shift is over."

Thirty minutes later, the wind changed directions. The intensity of a north wind developed. The pressure of the current pushed harder against the hull which forced a change in our heading.

I heard what sounded like breaking waves off our port side. I looked ahead and screamed, "Jim! Jim! Wake up!

There are breakers, and I see surf off the port side!" *Far Horizons* crashed into a reef. I was thrown from behind the helm and slammed against the cabin hatch. The yacht heeled sharply to port.

Jim struggled out of the aft cabin, rubbing his eyes. He pulled on his pants. He saw the white foam and yelled, "Let off the sails!" The shrouds had torn loose. We released the sails. Tremendous waves pushed the yacht up, then slammed it down on the reef. We slipped on life jackets, and grasped the safety rail. Jim and I struggled to keep from being thrown overboard. The yacht pitched violently. The keel pounded on the reef with every wave.

"Children, wake up! Put on life jackets," I yelled into the hatchway. "Stay in the cabin where it's safe."

Alan jumped up from his berth, and called to his sister, "Alicia! Alicia! Wake up! We're in trouble. I'm putting my life jacket on. Put yours on now. Stay near me!"

It was a dark night with no visible lights in any direction. I held onto the helm again. Our clothes were drenched with sea water. I shivered from the wind. A song of joy burst forth in a new spontaneous prayer language that I didn't understand. It was a glad song that soared into the darkness. Hope arose in my heart. There wasn't any city or land in sight. Our yacht which had been our home for three years was being destroyed. Peace that could only come from Jesus ruled my heart. The impossible was subject to change. My heart had complete trust that God maintained control.

Alan asked, "Where is a harbor or a lighthouse? Will we be safe?"

"Stay in the main cabin with your sister. We'll let you know what to do next."

I questioned, "Jim, how long will our yacht hold together? Why isn't there a lighthouse?" The waves drenched our clothes as we shivered from exhaustion.

Jim replied, "It's time to launch the Dyer rubber raft! Put photographs and food in a five gallon plastic container and seal the lid. Put the container in the Dyer raft." I packed the container and placed it in the raft.

I prayed, "Father, please send the right person to find and open this container, to see our family photographs and come to help us."

I helped him toss the raft over the port side. Jim resisted thrashing waves as he secured the raft. The yacht lurched and plunged back and forth on the reef.

Jim called out an emergency distress message via the VHF radio, "May Day! May Day!" He repeated this call over and over. No one responded.

The Dyer raft line broke away and disappeared about two o'clock in the morning with our photographs and food. He groaned, "Oh, no, our Dyer raft broke loose. It must have disappeared during the night!"

Jim instructed, "Elsie, let's put the fiberglass dinghy over the side and secure it with a line." We launched the fiberglass dinghy and secured it with a small line to a cleat.

Jim directed, "Elsie, store emergency supplies in another plastic container. Seal it and put this one in the fiberglass dinghy."

After I packed more food and emergency supplies, I sealed the second container. "Jim, it's ready. I've tied a line around the handle of the container." I placed the container in the fiberglass dinghy and secured the line.

A big wave jerked the yacht to port. Jim shouted, "I've got to put our two oars and oarlocks in the fiberglass dinghy!" He leaned over the side. "Oh, God, I lost both oars and the oarlocks overboard when the wave hit!"

Nine hours passed as our yacht slammed continuously on the reef. As dawn peeked over the horizon, Jim took a survey of our situation.

Alicia sat huddled on the floor of the galley with her life jacket on. She shivered in fear. Her eyes opened wide and she stood. "Mom, there's sea water flooding into the galley! Where can I go? What should I do?" The pounding on the reef had cracked our fiberglass hull.

Jim commanded, "Start bailing! Everyone start bailing!" We all grabbed buckets of different sizes. The children and I scooped sea water from the galley floor. We passed the buckets out the hatch. Jim tossed the sea water overboard. He threw the empty buckets back to us. The wind howled and the waves threatened to overturn our yacht.

Jim tried to use the large emergency pump. He gulped. "The pump's not working. I can't seem to fix it."

Alan called, "Mom, now there's sea water pouring under the table area in the main cabin! It's coming in faster!"

"Elsie, get flares ready. Everyone put on long pants, long-sleeved shirts and sneakers. Skin won't be torn on coral if we're overturned. Kids, we'll all work together." Jim seemed to have a sensible plan.

I prepared the children first, and got the flare gun and flares ready.

After daylight came, a section of the yacht floated past the port side. Jim pointed, "Look, it's our broken rudder! Oh, no! We're finished." We watched as a large piece of our yacht with the rudder attached passed by our port side.

"We'll have to abandon ship," Jim said in a final tone. He dropped his head in defeat. "It's time to get the emergency Avon inflatable raft off from the coach roof in front of the mast. Elsie, hang on to the safety line and grab rails on the coach roof. Crawl on your hands and knees after me." I followed him. Our home on the yacht was being destroyed while peace reigned in my heart.

Jim and I crawled single file and reached the white fiberglass-encased raft and dragged it back to the cockpit. We struggled to keep from being thrown overboard. Jim unstrapped the white rectangular cover off of the case and unpacked the raft. Jim said, "I hope it inflates. It's our only chance."

Jim insisted, "Together we'll make *sure* this line is tied securely to our yacht. We'll toss it over the port side before we inflate the raft." We watched the round, orange-covered Avon raft as it fully inflated. We looked at each other and uttered sighs of relief.

I pressed, "It looks so small. We've never used it. Will we all fit into it? Will it tip over? Jim, I'm scared. The children are exhausted." I felt helpless.

Jim gave the word, "Save the compass and the two small fire extinguishers. Put the emergency medical kit, passports, money and business papers into the Avon raft. Keep your life jackets on. Elsie, get our children in the raft first. You get in next. I'll be in front in our hard dinghy."

I obeyed his orders. *Why does he need to take the large box of business papers with us?* The children and I climbed into the circular raft with the bright orange top and door flap. Jim stepped into the fiberglass dinghy. He leaned over and tied a line between our rafts. He mounted our tiny outboard motor on the hard dinghy. He pulled the starter cord several times in vain. He lamented, "It's not working." He shook his head.

We drifted and watched *Far Horizons* flounder with her last breath. She started to sink. I caught my breath and covered my mouth. I gasped, "Our home …"

"Lord, where is a shoreline? How long can we survive without any oars? Our motor doesn't work! We don't have any type of radio. How can we contact anyone?" My heart sank as I tried to think of a solution. "It's only you, Lord Jesus, who can get us help."

The children and I kept our eyes on Jim in the other dinghy. Alan said, "We can't lose sight of Dad. Where is a lighthouse?" We were stranded. Our life raft bobbed on the waves.

I pleaded, "Dear Lord, please keep our line connected so we don't drift apart and lose our family."

The kids peeked out the orange flap on our raft. Alan shouted, "Dad, look there's a canoe coming!" Jim waved both arms.

I reflected, "This *is* an answer to my prayer! Thank You, my heavenly Father."

We all clapped our hands and shouted, "Hooray! Hooray!"

A Kuna Indian man appeared in a large dugout canoe with an outboard motor. He attached a rope to the lead dinghy and pulled us behind his wooden dugout canoe. We motored slowly back to his island, San Ignacio de Tupile. He said, "Teng-a-mal-o. Neuedi." We couldn't understand what he said. This sounded like a greeting.

I was concerned, "Do we dare get out on their land? I hope they're friendly."

Dozens of Kuna Indians were on shore and stared at our strange emergency raft as we approached their island. Brave Alan asked, "Mom, who are these people?"

A different man cried, "Tenga mahl o, neuedi."

I tried to comfort the children, "They're Kuna Indians. A smile is universal. That's it, let's smile and hope it works." We poked our heads out of the orange flapped door of the raft, and smiled. Rows of Indians stood on shore with their dark olive toes curled over wooden logs. There were only puzzled looks but no smiles on the faces of the Kuna men.

"Kids, they're standing so close together. Where do we put our feet?" One Indian man tied the line from our life raft to shore to keep it from drifting away.

I started to get out of the raft, "What's left to lose?" The Indians moved apart to make a space for my feet. Alan and

Alicia, wearing their orange life jackets, stepped ashore after me.

A few Kuna women gathered around us. Alicia gasped, "Look at their large gold nose rings, Mom!" She clung to my hand.

Alan blurted out, "Mom, all the women's cheeks have red paint on them. What funny haircuts. All the same."

A colorful shawl covered their short black hair. The Indian women wore many beaded bands on their arms and legs. We had read information about these Indians a few weeks ago. The mola is a blouse decorated in the front and the back with layered patterns in reverse appliqué. The designs show the personality and express the woman's feelings. Black coal tar makeup is used to draw attention to the length of nose with a line drawn down the center of a woman's nose.

Our family of four huddled together in a state of shock. I was stunned. Constant stress, lack of sleep and the ordeal of the violence at sea overpowered me. I was emotionally devastated. My bones and muscles ached from the severe pounding on the reef all night long.

Questions flooded my mind. *What are these people saying? I can't understand their language. Are they friendly? Will they help us? How are we going to get back to the states?*

Chapter 19

Gather Up the Fragments

The village consisted of palm-thatched huts with dirt floors. Jim and I followed our rescuer into the only small frame building. This Kuna man pointed to a twin bed, and indicated with his hand that Jim and I were to share that bed. Alicia followed a Kuna woman to a separate thatched hut. Alan used a small cot in the room next to us. I was in a daze. The children clenched their lips and stared at the Indians.

I salvaged my small devotional book and read aloud: "… Gather up the fragments that nothing be lost."

We collected what we could as items were brought to shore. We put small things into three five-gallon plastic pails with white lids. One pail was green and the other two were white. Two canvas sea bags were rescued. Our family of four huddled together in a state of shock. Our home on *Far Horizons* was lost.

I wept and shrieked through the night in fitful dreams. *Where am I? What happened? Where are my children? Where's my husband? We're sinking! We're hitting a reef. Help!* I screamed for help, "Someone help us!" I was delirious.

The next morning, we knew that our food supplies had sunk or floated away. Diesel fuel stained our clothing and other belongings. The Kuna men gathered in their dugout canoes. They raced to salvage what they could from our yacht. Each man paddled his canoe filled with our items to their island of San Ignacio de Tupile. Our family's belongings, clothing, dishes, sewing items, books and navigational charts were scattered throughout the village. We watched as fragments of our yacht, parts of the coach roof, and the hull were brought into the village and scattered at random.

The salvaging continued all day with trips back and forth. The sandwiched part of fiberglass, wood and fiberglass sections of our yacht filled the dirt yard. I couldn't believe this was happening. It had to be a dream.

I screamed many times during that night from severe shock. I called out to Jim, "Help, we're sinking! Where are our children?"

The next day, Jim and I woke up and opened the pole shutters. To our surprise, numerous Kuna Indians stood outside the open windows. They stared at us without speaking any words. Jim spoke, "We're on exhibition. It's like being in a zoo. Pull yourself together. Elsie, let's find the children first." He was calm.

I was drained, "Where are we?" I covered my body with a sheet, got up and closed the shutters. I put on my ragged shorts, a tank top and my yellow sneakers. There were torn holes on top of each sneaker. I searched for a pair of shoelaces and found one pair. I inserted the shoelaces into the eyelets of the sneakers. With gratitude I breathed, "Thank You, Lord, for these shoelaces!" With straggled hair and a sunburned face, I asked, "Jim, how we will ever get back to the United States.?" He didn't answer.

Jim said, "Alan, let's ride out on one of the canoes to see what we can salvage. If we dive under the sea water, it's possible to get inside our yacht. Stay close to me."

Alan took a deep breath. "Okay, Dad, I'm ready."

Jim and Alan rode out in a canoe with a Kuna man to the location where our yacht had sunk. Alan reported, "Mom, I swam inside the galley and main cabin. I put some things inside the Indian's canoe to bring back for you. He disappeared with his canoe and now I don't know which Indian it was!" Jim came back empty-handed.

Antonia Oran, a short, gray-haired Kuna woman walked into our room. She reached for my hand and held it. She could not speak English, but I spoke, "Jim, she reminds me of my stepmother. She never could tell me that she loved me, but she expressed her concern by being there for me." My heart was comforted by this strange woman. She wore a gold nose ring. Her nose had black lines drawn down the center of her entire nose. Antonia's cheeks were painted with a red color. Her hair was black and cut short below her ears. She wore an orange scarf over her head. Her dress was primitive with a decorative hand-stitched design of brilliant colors.

The following morning, Antonia and I walked throughout the village. She introduced me to her family members and friends in her language and gestures. She brought me to the hut where my daughter, Alicia, was sleeping in a hammock. There was an orange and white kitten beside her. With tears in my eyes I prayed, "Thank You, Lord, for your care for us and to have given Alicia a kitten to comfort her."

I found my little devotional book and read, *"The Lord shall preserve thee from all evil: he shall preserve thy soul. The Lord shall preserve thy going out and thy coming in from this time forth, and even for evermore."*

Cooking was done over five logs in a thatched hut. Each family had two huts; one for cooking and the other for sleeping in hammocks. Jim called to us, "Come and eat. The Indians cooked a meal for us. It's in the thatched cooking hut in back."

A young Kuna woman, Noelia, shredded fresh coconut and then put the coconut into rice. Our family watched the embers burn on the five logs. Small fish were cooked in a pan over these logs. Noelia fanned the fire to turn the heat up. Later, she pulled the logs apart to lower the heat when she was done cooking. I took a bite and said, "What a delicious bowl of rice. This is good food. I never thought to shred fresh coconut into rice." Jim and the children gobbled up their food. We were hungry.

Alicia asked, "Guess what I did today?"

Jim and I responded, "What did you do today?"

"I saw a bottle of ketchup floating in the water. I swam out and brought it to shore." She smiled. "It must have been one of ours."

"What? Don't go in the ocean unless we're with you!" We cringed.

I used blank pages from our Guest Log in order to continue my journal.

On another morning, we were served eggs cooked over an open fire in the cooking hut. "What a nice surprise. These eggs must have come from our tiny ice chest in our galley," Jim declared. Both huts have dirt floors which are swept with a broom. The house goes to the girl. The women were out in the daytime. The men were out at night.

Later that morning, I darted down a narrow dirt path, past several thatched huts. I wanted to be alone. I was still in a daze from our shipwreck four days earlier. It was a lovely, sunny day. The sky was clear. These Indians were so different from any I'd seen in the United States. I was surprised to see two Indian men who balanced on each end of a long tree limb. Underneath the center of the tree limb was a large bucket. An Indian woman watched the bucket to see if the cane stalks were crushed enough by the rounded piece of wood in the center. The process continued back and forth like a teeter-totter.

As I rounded the next turn on the path, a Kuna woman rushed out of a hut. She grabbed my arm, and pulled me alongside of her. Her face expressed concern. She needed help. I questioned, "What's wrong? Where are we going?" The Kuna woman couldn't speak English. She led me to a large thatched hut. We went inside the hut. She handed me a tiny baby girl. I asked, "Is the baby sick? " I felt the baby's forehead, and uncovered her chest. I looked at her arms and legs. "There aren't any spots. I don't feel any fever. Does she need prayer?" The woman gawked at me. She didn't understand what I was saying.

I collapsed in the one chair in the hut. I wailed urgent prayers for this baby girl. Other Indians entered the hut and stared at me. When I felt a release in prayer, I got up to leave. *What do I do next?* One man, Faustino, burst into the hut. He was the only Kuna that I met who spoke English. He interpreted, "Baby sick, witch doctor come tonight. Come every night."

Faustino pulled several carved wooden fetishes out of a cloth bag. Some were shaped like large fish, a revolver, or animals. He explained, "These are used to ward off sickness. Each family keeps their fetishes in a cloth bag." A few days before, I had been in this large hut. I sighted several primitive carved wooden figures on a shelf. They were approximately eighteen inches tall. The wood was light in color and the bodies of the wooden figures had never been stained. I asked, "What are these wooden figures with red stained hair?" I innocently thought they were decorations.

Faustino warned, "Witch doctor say ... no touch, you die!" Then he turned and explained, "Over here behind this curtain is a trough filled with herbs and water. A woman and her baby will be in the hammock for eight days. A witch doctor will be here tonight. You can come to see witch doctor – you woman. No men are allowed in the hut."

Now these carved wooden idols were placed on the dirt floor in a definite order. Green sticks with twisted reeds were alongside the red-haired idols. The reeds looked like a fancy cross with a cup-like top. Faustino said, "They will call on Jesus Christ for four hours every night from 6:30 P.M. to 10:30 P.M." This was a form of religion mixed with witchcraft.

I answered, "Faustino, I have to ask Jesus Christ, and also my husband about tonight. I don't think either of them would want me to come here tonight. I believe that Jesus is the Healer."

Shaking inside, I walked out of the hut. *What am I supposed to do? How can I get out of this difficult situation? We're intruders on this island.* I walked slowly as if nothing had happened.

Jim met me by the shore. He was picking up coconuts. He walked toward me. He questioned, "What's wrong? Why are you trembling?"

I blurted out, "I wandered through the village. A woman came out of a hut, grabbed my arm and led me to her hut. She handed me a baby. I couldn't understand her. The only man who spoke English told me the baby is sick. The witch doctor's coming tonight to their hut." I gasped for air.

Jim ordered, "You're not going there tonight. Stay with the family." I nodded and sighed with relief.

After our evening meal, our family stayed in the cooking hut to talk. The adult Indians disappeared. Our family sat on the wooden plank bench and watched the embers burn on the five logs. Little Kuna children filled the hut. I volunteered, "Jim, are we babysitting? Can't very well leave the children alone, could we?"

Jim came up with an idea. He pointed to a small boy. Jim demonstrated, "This child sits by us. Now cover your eyes with your hands." He showed the boy how to cover his eyes. The other children lined up on the long bench by the side wall of the thatched hut. Jim pointed to one little girl. He made a sound like a kitten, "Meow."

The little girl copied his sound, "Meow, meow."

Then with his eyes covered, the boy guessed who had made the sound. He pointed to the girl. They exchanged seats. If a child was wrong, someone else meowed. The children loved this game. The evening spent with the Kuna children was over. I was relieved that it was time to go to bed.

The next day, Alan sketched a picture of a sailboat. He wrote on the paper: DEATH of FAR HORIZONS. March 9th, 1979. He handed it to us. Tears ran down his cheeks. He seemed nervous, bitter, and had been having trouble sleeping. We were all stressed and in a state of shock.

There were two meals a day. For breakfast we were served coconuts, coffee, and mashed plantain. The coffee must have been salvaged from our yacht. For the early evening meal we had rice, cooked fish, and plantain.

Joe gave Jim a wooden idol to drive demons away. Antonia gave me a Kuna Indian necklace with matching shells plus a handmade mola on a black cloth background with four birds and bright colors with a tree design. A mola is a unique intricately appliqué technique in which tiny pieces of cotton cloth are sewn on to a cut-work cloth base.

We looked toward the ocean. Jim shouted, "They've rescued what's left of our coach roof and hull." Indians paddled the remains into their village. I grabbed our camera and returned singing in the Holy Spirit through the village. *Would there be anything left?*

A Kuna man talked to Jim in what sounded like Spanish. This was different from the Kuna language. We saw two nuns in a different part of the island, so we gave them the few medical supplies that had been salvaged.

Parts of our yacht and cabin supplies were strung all over the village in various huts. Alan's brown jib was flying on a pole in front of a hut. My light green, wool cape was hanging on a line by a different hut. My sunglasses were returned.

March 11th: Faustino Oran received Jesus! He told Eleuterio, Antonia, and several children. I gave him my Bible. His wife gave me a shell necklace also, and a mola with five flowers stitched on a red background. His wife didn't speak English.

March 12th

Jim and I went in Eleuterio's long, dugout canoe to see the coconut trees which were separated by a line of palm branches. We saw an old woman swinging her machete at a coconut tree. Coconut trees seemed to be the Kunas form of wealth. "Oh, look, there are lime trees!" I exclaimed. We climbed a scraggly hill choked with plants and bushes.

The following evening, our family was invited to attend their Congress. This was held in the largest hut in the village. The chief of the village was Ignacio Smith. Two old men sat in hammocks in the center of the hut and sang chants. Other Indians sat on benches. One Kuna man sat on a bench near the chanting men in the hammocks. He held a large wooden bat. Should someone fall asleep, this man would wave the bat at the sleeper as a warning. It seemed as if the two men were relating stories or legends from their ancestors. They took turns in their folk song.

Faustino said, "We must attend Congress on Sunday and Wednesday night or we can't leave the island. Must cut grass by airfield or fined fifty cents. We work hard, be good, and will go to heaven. We bring all Kuna problems to chief and he settles them. All help build hut. Wild boars in mountain."

In the afternoon, I walked outside the hut. I wonder what this day would bring. A different mother carried a baby. The baby's body was covered gray ashes. She walked toward me several times. *I wonder why she keeps coming near me?* She couldn't speak English so I couldn't ask her any questions.

Later, Faustino, with a surprised look on his face reported, "The baby girl that you saw yesterday is well."

"Thank you, Lord Jesus, for healing that baby girl."

"Jim, how are we going to get back to the United States? Have you heard of any boat or ship coming to this island that will give us a ride?" I paused and hoped that he had found a solution.

Chapter 20

Waves of Hope

March 13th 1979

Jim packed our emergency inflatable raft and two fire extinguishers into sea bags. I used the plastic paint buckets with covers (that had held our rice, sugar and flour) for our luggage. Kuna Indian men gathered around our family as we waited for a motor vessel to arrive from Columbia. It was scheduled once a week for a ten minute stop. The Indian mothers watched us as they held children in their arms.

Markland was a medium-sized wooden Columbian island avocado schooner with an inboard diesel motor. It pulled up to the dock. The schooner captain, a middle-aged bearded man, stepped onto the dock. Jim walked up to him and introduced himself. "I'm Jim MacGregor. This is my family. We need passage for my wife and our two children."

The captain answered, "I'm Captain Cuevas. What do you have to trade?"

Jim replied, "I'll trade a compass and two fire extinguishers."

Captain Cuevas requested, "Let me examine them." He checked the extinguishers. He continued, "Get on board.

We leave now." Our family boarded *Markland* and waved goodbye to the Kunas who gathered on the dock at two-thirty in the afternoon. Other passengers crowded aboard the schooner. We found a spot where we sat back to back with the Kuna Indians on top of wooden storage containers.

Alicia complained, "We're crushed. No place to hold."

Alan said, "Be glad for a place to sit. Mom and Dad, I love you."

Alicia volunteered, "I love you too. Alan, you're not so bad either."

Captain Cuevas handed Alan and Alicia an avocado. He gave avocados and a knife to Jim. Jim said, "Thanks. We're hungry."

It was a three hour trip from San Ignacio de Tupile to Provenir. In the evening we got off the schooner at Porvenir village and rented a tiny room at a small hotel. There wasn't any water in the room and there weren't any towels. The room was ten dollars a night for four, including dinner and a breakfast meal.

March 14th

We saw *Quest* with Chuck and Vann. We had met them on December 30th of 1978 in Bequia, West Indies. Jim asked, "Where are you headed? We lost our yacht and there's a large sea bag that needs to be shipped to us in California. Would you take it with you?"

Chuck volunteered, "Yes, we're working our way back to Corona, California."

March 16th 1979

Cisne, a dirty old boat packed with Kuna Indians, checked into Porvenir. The captain was a sweaty fat man. Jim bargained, "We need passage to Colon for the four of us. I'll trade this sail bag with an inflatable life raft for our fare."

Captain Pineda responded, "This will work. We leave Porvenir at seven-thirty in the morning."

We were now down to four buckets, one sea bag, a small overnight case and my purse. I prayed with Alan and Alicia then read: [14] And he said, 'My presence shall go with thee, and I will give thee rest.' Ex 33:14 KJV

Our seat was a wooden plank, one foot wide and stretched across the open hatches on each side of the boat. This plank was one foot above the deck without any back rest. The boat creaked and groaned as it shifted from side to side with the motion of the waves. Alan observed, "Look at the Indians. They're seasick." Several Kunas sat on the opposite end of the plank. They held their stomachs as they bent over the side and vomited.

Our meager belongings bounced up and down in front of us in the plastic buckets and sea bag. We hugged each other. I said, encouragingly, "We'll make it, kids. One step, one day at a time. We'll work our way back to California."

Jim poked at a large shape that sat to our right. He lifted a red cloth that covered it. He gasped, "Oh, God! Look under this fuel stained cloth. It's our engine head and oil filter parts from *Far Horizons*!"

I winced, "Part of our yacht riding with us on this schooner! Oh, no! They're going to sell it."

Jim showed the kids our former engine. The old boat rocked back and forth, side to side on every wave. I marveled, "The engine salvaged and being sent to Colon? What next? Is this filthy boat going to hold together? The way the boards groan and shift ...."

We arrived in Colon, Panama in the evening. We disembarked and walked to a guard station. There were several Panamanian soldiers who stood around it. Jim found one empty bench. He said, "Elsie, you and the kids sit here and wait for me. Looks like you'll be safe with these soldiers nearby. I'll find out about a train."

About five minutes after Jim left, all the soldiers disappeared. The children and I huddled together. Alan wondered, "When's dad coming back? We're worried. It's getting dark."

Alicia complained, "We're hungry, Mom"

I said flatly, "Your dad will come to get us. He wouldn't leave us stranded in a strange country."

Out of the dark Jim walked under trees toward us. He said, "We'll walk to the train station. It's not too far. I'll carry the sail bag and one of the buckets." He showed us the train tickets. We walked to the train station and got on a train toward Panama City, Panama. The train jolted often as it sped down the track. I said softly, "This ride hurts my muscles. I'm still sore from the shipwreck." It was a one hour train ride.

We took a bus to Hotel Ideal and checked in for the night. The next day our family walked into Jim Murphy's office, who was the current American Ambassador. Alan exclaimed, "How great to see our American flag!"

The ambassador stood and offered his hand to each of us. Jim smiled and said, "How do you do, Mr. Ambassador. I'm Jim MacGregor. This is my wife, Elsie. Alan and Alicia are our children."

Jim Murphy extended his hand and said, "Welcome to Panama. How may I be of service?"

Jim related, "Our yacht sank off the coast of San Ignacio de Tupile. We didn't enter through normal areas, so exit permits have been denied. Can you help us return to the United States?"

The ambassador intervened, "I'll write a letter in Spanish to explain what has happened to your yacht and your family. This will open the door for you to clear Panamanian customs." He immediately sat at his desk, wrote the letter, and handed it to Jim. He concluded, "I wish you and your family well and a safe trip back to the United States. Goodbye."

In the morning the American Ambassador took us to a cheaper place, Pensione du Mexico. "You'll need to stay here until you are granted exit permits to leave Panama."

March 18th

I realized I'd lost all my recipes for the past twenty-three years, food, books, clothing, wedding rings, and jewelry. Alan piped up, "I lost my guitar, watch and my books. But we have our lives."

March 19th

We took a taxi to the airport where Jim bought four tickets to Miami, Florida. Our family looked bedraggled. Alicia had grown and needed her own passport. Current photos were taken before we were given new passports. We were charged eight dollars a person for airline service before we were allowed on a Braniff Airlines plane.

A hot meal was served to our family. I relaxed. "It's a luxury to sit on a plane with comfortable seats."

Alan rejoiced, "Dad, Mom, my seat reclines! Wow, this is neat. A headset for a radio? Soda pop ... for me?"

Alicia sighed and said, "I'm going to take a nice nap at last."

The flight was good. I still wore my yellow sneakers with the holes in the toes. These were my only shoes. I commented, "I know that we all look a mess with hair that needs cutting and worn-out clothes." When we arrived in the baggage area, passengers gawked at our sea bag, and the three plastic five-gallon pails with lids.

We took a cab to Jim's Aunt Ella and Uncle Dave's home. We hugged each other.

Aunt Ella said, "The first thing we're going to do is to buy shoes for the children. Then shoes for you, Elsie, and some safe shoes for you, too, Jim."

I reported, "Ella, I managed to save the diary that you gave me. I've taken notes in pencil the entire time."

Ella fussed over our children. She fixed a grand dinner with steak, French fries, and salad. Alan grinned and proclaimed, "French fries! Aunt Ella, we haven't had French fries since we left the United States. A feast!"

I eyed the washing machine and dryer. Another luxury. Our family's clothing was worn and ragged. I hung my head and tried not to cry. Alicia blurted, "Oh, my God! It's a T.V."

Alan shouted, "Mom, hot water!" Culture shock slapped us.

Jim announced, "We have one more effort to reach California. Trailways bus should be the cheapest way to travel. I'll get our tickets tomorrow."

The next day, we waved goodbye to Ella and Dave as we boarded the Trailways bus. Our kids chose different seats where they could stretch out to sleep. It took three days to get to Colleyville, Texas where we visited Connie and Phil Harris and their two girls, Cathy and Debbie. What a joy to have returned safely!

In the evening, I went to Calvary Cathedral with Connie. Bob Nichols was the pastor. At the end of the service, I went to the altar for prayer. All I could do was scream several times as the stress and tension poured out. Many people in the congregation rushed forward to pray for me. I was exhausted.

We stayed overnight. The next morning, the children went outside and played in the backyard. I had prayer time with Connie and her mother, Dorothy Hollander. My prayer language was released and overflowed. First, I poured my burdens out; second, I did warfare in the spirit; third, the comfort of the Holy Spirit completed the release. There was wonderful fellowship as Connie, Dorothy, and I laughed together in the victory of our Lord.

It was another three day bus journey from Texas to California. Dick and Mary Wilson welcomed us with open arms when we arrived at the bus station in Hayward. Mary fixed us a hot meal and invited us to stay with them overnight.

Jim's sister, Joan Branch and her husband, Russ offered their RV which was parked in their backyard for us to use while we looked for an apartment to rent. We were grateful for this offer.

I commented, "My goal has been reached. Our children are safe. None of us were seriously injured. Yes, we lost our yacht, which had become our home. Thank You, Lord Jesus, for your safekeeping. I love you."

GLOSSARY

Aft cabin – the cabin at the stern or end of the yacht

Aerial flare – pistol launched flare to show a yacht's location when in danger

Barnacle – a hard crust or shell, a crustacean; in the adult stage it attaches itself permanently to a rock or a ship's hull

Beam – widest part of the yacht

Berth – a place to sleep (main berth, V- berth, Quarter berth)

Boom – a spar extending from a mast to hold the bottom of a mainsail outstretched and capable of swinging across the yacht.

Boom vang – block and tackle that holds a boom down and prevents the sail from twisting.

Bo' sun chair – a heavy canvas seat for a crew member to be hauled aloft (up) to check or repair the rigging.

Bow – the front part of a yacht

Careened - to lean on one side

Cay - a low island, coral reef or sandbank off a mainland

Chart – a navigational map used to chart a course on the oceans.

Chart table – provides space to spread out the navigational charts.

Cockpit – the sunken area on deck where the crew sits.

Companionway - stairs from the cockpit going below deck.

Danforth – a type of anchor

Dinghy – a small boat carried on a yacht

Draft – the depth of a vessel below the waterline

Fathom – six feet

Fathom – a nautical measure equal to six feet, for measuring water depths, or lengths of lead lines, cordage, and anchor chains

Fathometer – a type of echo sounder

Galley – a small kitchen on a boat, yacht, ship

Genoa – a large jib or headsail set on the forestay.

Halyard – line used to hoist a sail

Heel – angle of a yacht when it leans to one side while sailing

Jibe – to turn a yacht's stern through the wind so that the sails swing from one side of the yacht to the other, putting the yacht on another tack.

Knot – a nautical mile or 1.15 statute miles

Port Side – the left hand side of the yacht while facing toward the bow

Reefed – to reduce sail area as the wind increased

Reef points – reinforced grommets in a sail. Line is tied through these to gather the loose sail.

RDF – radio direction finder A specialized marine radio capable of establishing the bearing of the station whose signal it is receiving.

Safety belt – a six inch wide belt attached to eyebolts at each end of counter worn in the galley when underway.

Sextant – an instrument used by navigators for measuring the angular distance of the sun, a star from the horizon, to find the position of a ship

Shroud – a stay running from the side of the boat to the side of the mast. Provides lateral support for the mast.

Stanchion – an upright bar, beam or post used as a support

Starboard side – the right hand side of the yacht while facing toward the bow

Stay – any wire or line that supports a mast

Stern – the aft or rear of the yacht

Storm jib – a small flat-cut jib for use in strong weather

Tacking – a change of direction when the sails shift from one side of the vessel to another to maneuver a vessel against the wind by a series of tacks.

VHF – a very high frequency for radio transmission A designated band of the radio spectrum ranging from 30 to 300 MHz.

Wake – the churned up water behind the yacht that marks its course

CPSIA information can be obtained at www.ICGtesting.com
Printed in the USA
LVOW080007080312

272132LV00002B/1/P